THE PINK BOOK **2014**

Legislation

for tourist accommodation

Published by VisitEngland,
Sanctuary Buildings,
20 Great Smith Street,
London, SW1P 3BT
Publishing Manager: Ross Calladine

Written and edited by Kurt Janson Ltd
Cover design and typsetting by Carrington Griffin Design

Legislation for Tourist Accommodation

Welcome to the 2014 edition of VisitEngland's *Pink Book: Legislation for tourist accommodation*.

Published seven times previously, the Pink Book has always been recognised as providing significant support to the tourism sector. It provides a common sense approach to helping accommodation providers understand their complex and often daunting legal obligations.

The guidance contained here is also available online at **www.visitengland.com/pinkbookonline** – this is updated as legislation changes.

Keeping up to date with legislation

If you run a tourism accommodation business of any kind (including self-catering) or are involved with running or advising tourism accommodation businesses, you need to be aware of the legislation that applies to such businesses.

There is a wide range of applicable legislation. Guests are increasingly demanding higher quality and are becoming more aware of their rights. Complying with legislative requirements helps you to meet these expectations and avoid claims, prosecution and fines.

This book provides practical guidance on the legislation relevant to accommodation providers in England. (For legislation relevant to those outside England, please contact the relevant National Tourist Board).

Using the book

This book is arranged into eight main sections, as follows, each of which contains a number of topics. Page tabs have been provided to help you quickly reach the section you need:

- Licences & Consents
- Marketing
- Guests
- Food & Drink

- Health & Safety
- Staff
- Business Management & Tax
- Further Information

The final section, 'Further Information', provides details of where to go for further help and a list of useful websites and definitions.

See the Contents page or **www.visitengland.com/pinkbookonline** for an immediate pointer to these main sections and topics or go to the Index at the back of the book for an alphabetical listing of the subjects and legislation covered.

Legislation which has been updated since the 7th edition of the Pink Book (published 2012) is identified by an 'Updated' tab in the margin. These updates are correct as of July 2014.

Please note

While every effort has been made to ensure the accuracy of the information contained in this booklet, it is intended to be an introductory guide only. It is not intended to be comprehensive or a definitive statement of the law in England. If you require precise or detailed information on the legislation mentioned in this guide, or on the legal implications for you in particular, you should consult a professional legal adviser.

Please note also that as part of the day-to-day workings of the government, all policy areas continue to be subject to review, update and amendments. Elements of the information explained here may be subject to revision – updates to legislation will be posted online, but if in any doubt you should always check with the relevant authorities.

Welcome to the 2014 Edition
of the *Pink Book*

Tourism small and medium enterprises (SMEs) are extremely important to the UK economy. One of the first things that the Government did when it was elected was to realise that for the economy to recover, we needed to support small businesses. As well as lowering business tax rates and introducing an exemption from business rates for SMEs, we realised that one of the best ways to provide support was to reduce regulatory burden.

In addition to holding a national Red Tape Challenge, which had a specific Hospitality and Tourism section, the Department for Culture, Media and Sport also convened a Ministerial working group to develop recommendations on legislation that could be amended or repealed in order to help tourism businesses.

The department is now working through this detailed report and, as a result, significant changes are being made that will reduce the time that SMEs have to spend on compliance. I am very pleased that we have managed to reduce some of the red tape that affects the tourism industry including reducing requirements for no-smoking signage, removing some redundant health and safety legislation and simplifying food safety regulations.

We are also in the process of introducing a new Community and Ancillary Sales Notice that will allow accommodation businesses to sell small amounts of alcohol without having to go through the costly process of applying for a full licence just to be able to provide customers with a glass of wine with their meal.

There is more to do, but we are making considerable progress in partnership with the industry and I am excited by the opportunities to further develop the UK tourism industry in 2015, including hosting the Rugby World Cup and celebrating the 800th anniversary of the Magna Carta.

Helen Grant MP *Minister for Tourism*

Contents

LICENCES & CONSENTS

MARKETING

GUESTS

FOOD & DRINK

HEALTH & SAFETY

STAFF

BUSINESS MANAGEMENT & TAX

FURTHER INFORMATION

Alcohol and Entertainment Licensing

KEY FACTS

- If you wish to sell alcoholic drinks you will need a licence.
- There are two types of licence: premises licences and personal licences.

Does the legislation apply to me?

If you wish to sell alcoholic drinks you will need an alcohol licence. It is an offence to sell alcohol without one.

Providing 'free' alcohol to guests

You need a licence to sell alcohol – selling includes providing 'free' alcohol because it is an incentive to purchase and is included in your pricing structure. The fact that you charge the guest for staying in your accommodation means that they are essentially paying for the alcohol that is provided. In other words, the guest has effectively paid a 'consideration' for that service. It is not free.

Note: the Government is currently in the process of introducing Community and Ancillary Sales Notices (CANs), which will allow accommodation businesses to sell small amounts of alcohol for a nominal fee. These are expected to be introduced in late 2015.

In addition, the Government is introducing other changes to licensing requirements, including devolving licensing fee setting to the local level, removing the need for personal licences and strengthening mandatory licensing conditions. These changes are included in the Deregulation Bill that is currently before Parliament and should be introduced in early 2015.

The Licensing Act 2003

The **Licensing Act 2003** rationalised the previous various licensing systems (in England and Wales) to produce a simpler system that is easier for all involved to understand.

Local authorities are required to consult on their statement of licensing policy every three years. Before applying for a licence, it is therefore important for you to read this policy. This enables you to tailor your application to the licensing authority's policy to reduce the risk of the application being rejected.

Administration and enforcement

Administration and enforcement of the Licensing Act lies with local authorities (and other agencies where appropriate), e.g. fire safety, police, licensing officers and environmental health. Each local authority will have a licensing committee of between 10 and 15 locally-elected councillors who decide on licensing applications.

In practice, their responsibilities are devolved to a licensing manager and staff who deal with the administrative functions. All contested applications will be heard before a sub-committee of at least three members of that committee.

Licensing objectives

There are four principles which underpin the Licensing Act and impact on everyone. These are:
- the prevention of crime and disorder
- public safety
- the prevention of public nuisance
- the protection of children from harm.

These principles are the key elements to be addressed by applicants, local authorities, police and other statutory authorities, and objectors to your licence.

Licensable activities

Activities regulated by the Licensing Act 2003 fall into one of the following four categories:
- the sale of alcohol
- the supply of alcohol by or on behalf of a club
- provision of regulated entertainment
- provision of late night refreshments.

The activities which accommodation providers should be familiar with are as follows.

Provision of regulated entertainment

Regulated entertainment includes many of the activities offered for the benefit of your guests and customers in, for example, public houses, hotels, guest houses, club rooms at caravan parks, i.e.:

- dancing either as a show for customers or as an activity for them to take part in
- films (defined as any showing of moving pictures)
- plays
- all indoor sporting events (physical skills must be a factor)
- music – the public playing of recorded music (e.g. DJs) as an accompaniment to dancing. (See *Live Music Act 2012* below).

Provision of late night refreshment

Provision of late night refreshment covers the supply of hot food or drinks from premises for consumption on or off premises between 11pm and 5am. This aspect is mainly focused on late-night takeaway premises, so an exception is made for the provision of refreshments by hotels, guest houses, hostels and caravan sites.

If, however, you have a restaurant which serves hot food and drinks to members of the public after 11pm you will need to nominate this as one of your licensable activities. Should you have any doubts about what should be included as licensable activities, your local licensing authority will be able to give advice.

Types of licences

There are two licences.

- **Premises licence:** required for any premises that offer any of the licensable activities previously described.
- **Personal licence:** a separate, portable system of personal licences that provides authority to sell alcohol. A designated premises supervisor, who must be a personal licence holder, must be nominated for any premises where the licence includes permission to sell alcohol. In order to obtain a personal licence the applicant must:
  - be 18 or over
  - possess an accredited licensing qualification
  - not have forfeited a personal licence within five years of the application

  and
  - not have been convicted of any relevant offence.

Note: currently, a premises licence and a personal licence are both required to sell alcohol. Although a premises licence is indefinite, a personal licence is required to be renewed every 10 years. However, proposed changes to the Licensing Act should soon remove the requirement for a personal licence.

LICENCES & CONSENTS MARKETING GUESTS FOOD & DRINK HEALTH & SAFETY STAFF BUSINESS MANAGEMENT & TAX FURTHER INFORMATION

Temporary Event Notices (TENs)

A Temporary Event Notice (TEN) is a licence to hold one-off licensable activities in an unlicensed premises. You are limited to a maximum of five per year if you do not hold a personal licence and 50 if you do. No more than 12 TENs can be given in respect of any particular premises in any calendar year and each event covered by a TEN can only last up to 96 hours (to a maximum of 15 days per year in aggregate) and can only be attended by a maximum of 499 people. There must also be a minimum of 24 hours between events.

Note: the Government is currently introducing changes to the Licensing Act that will enable businesses to apply for 15 TENs per year rather than the current 12. This change should be introduced in 2015.

The Alcohol Licensing section of the Gov.uk website **www.gov.uk/alcohol-licensing** offers information related to the Licensing Act and the application process.

Applying for a premises licence

Your application must embrace the four licensing objectives and you will need to assess any risks associated with each activity you propose to offer.

Advice can be obtained from the relevant statutory authority to achieve this, e.g. fire safety officer in respect of means of escape under the public safety objective. The police may require CCTV or door supervisors (usually for premises which stay open until the early hours) under the prevention of crime and disorder objective. Environmental health officers may offer advice on noise arising from any associated music under the prevention of public nuisance objective.

All statutory authorities and your neighbours/local businesses must also confine themselves to the four licensing objectives if they make any representation or objections.

Application process

Applications are made to the local licensing authority where the premises are located. The forms are available from the local authority's website and can be downloaded for completion together with guidance notes.

While the forms are relatively straightforward, you may wish to engage the services of a specialist licensing solicitor or consultant to

LICENCES & CONSENTS

MARKETING

GUESTS

FOOD & DRINK

HEALTH & SAFETY

STAFF

BUSINESS MANAGEMENT & TAX

FURTHER INFORMATION

UPDATED

assist you. The application can be made by anyone who undertakes, or proposes to undertake any business involving licensable activities. It includes limited companies or partnerships. If the application is made by an individual, that person must be at least 18 years of age.

You can apply for any of the licensable activities which are applicable to your business. Be mindful however, that you also have to serve a copy to the following statutory authorities:

- the Chief Officer of Police.
- the body recognised as responsible for the protection of children.
- Trading Standards officers.
- local planning authority.
- Environmental Health authority.
- Health and Safety authority.
- fire and rescue authority.

They will all wish to see that your premises and the activities you ask for are compatible.

For details of the responsible authorities in our area, contact your local licensing team. Details may also be available on your local authority's website.

Consultation

You are required to consult with your neighbours and local businesses in the area when seeking a licence or to vary an existing licence. This can be done by placing an advert in a local newspaper, setting out the brief details of your application and displaying a notice on your premises advertising details to passers-by. The guidance notes will give advice on these procedures.

The consultation process lasts for 28 days commencing on the day you submit the application to the local authority. Copies to the other authorities (mentioned above) must be served at the same time.

Providing there are no objections or representations that have not been resolved, the licensing authority will automatically issue your premises licence without you having to attend any meeting. Should there be any representations or objections which cannot be resolved by negotiation, the licensing authority will hold a hearing within 20 working days (from the end of the consultation period) to determine the application.

LICENSES & CONSENTS

LICENCES & CONSENTS · MARKETING · GUESTS · FOOD & DRINK · HEALTH & SAFETY · STAFF · BUSINESS MANAGEMENT & TAX · FURTHER INFORMATION

Fees

There are two sets of fees when applying for a premises licence. Both are based on rating bands and whether the primary or main purpose of the premises is to sell alcohol:

- the first fee is the cost to apply or to vary a licence.
- the second fee is the annual charge once the licence has been granted.

Once issued, the licence effectively lasts for as long as your business operates. The licence can be transferred from one licence holder to another. Again, the forms and guidance notes can be accessed on the local authority's website.

Variations to licences

Once a licence has been granted, licensees are required to operate within the conditions of the licence. If you would like a minor variation to these conditions, a simplified application process exists for this purpose. This process can only be used for variations that **could have no adverse impact on any of the four** *licensing objectives*.

For example, a Minor Variation Application could not be used in the following situations:

- to extend the period for which the licence or certificate has effect.
- to transfer the licence to other premises.
- to specify, in a premises licence, an individual as the premises supervisor.
- to add the sale by retail or supply of alcohol as an activity.
- to authorise the sale of alcohol at any time between 11pm and 7am.
- to authorise an increase in the amount of time on any day during which alcohol may be sold.

The cost of applying for a Minor Variation Application has been set at £89 and the maximum time that licensing authorities are able to take to process the application has been set at 15 days. Unlike a major variation to a licence, there is also no requirement to advertise or make other "responsible authorities", such as the police, aware of your intention to seek a minor variation.

Mandatory Code for the Sale of Alcohol

In addition to the Provisions of the Licensing Act, if you sell alcohol you are also required to comply with a Mandatory Code. This code:

- bans businesses from undertaking irresponsible promotions that encourage people to drink quickly or to drink more than they otherwise would. Examples include 'all you can drink for £10'

or 'free drinks when a football team scores'
- bans drinks being poured directly into customers mouths, i.e. 'dentist's chairs'
- requires operators to supply free tap water to customers
- requires businesses that sell alcohol to have an age-verification policy in place, and to check the ID of anyone who looks under 18
- requires businesses to sell alcohol in small measures (a half pint for beer and cider, 25ml or 35ml for spirits and 125ml for wine) as well as larger measures.
- bans the sale of alcohol below the "permitted price", which is defined as alcohol duty plus VAT.

How long can I stay open?

While the Licensing Act created the opportunity to stay open 24 hours, very few premises (with the exceptions of supermarkets) actually operate these hours. You can apply to have any of the licensable activities on your premises starting and finishing at any time to suit you and/or your customers.

Bear in mind that the statutory authorities and neighbours have to be notified and may not agree with your proposals. Common sense usually applies and many establishments have extended their operating hours by perhaps one or two hours.

Who can I sell alcohol to?

The old requirement for customers to be residents (or bona fide friends of residents or taking meals) no longer applies (provided these restrictions were not left on your licence when the new licensing regime started).

You can also decide at what age children are allowed into the licensed areas of your premises. Therefore babies and very young children can now be in your bar/restaurant, providing that they are accompanied by an adult.

Children aged 16 and 17 can also consume alcohol providing it is only beer, cider or wine, it has been purchased for them by an adult and it is taken with a table meal. The adult must be with the child at all times.

Live Music Act 2012

The Live Music Act exempts small licenced venues with audiences of up to 200 (including accommodation establishments, pubs, restaurants and community halls) from requiring a separate special licence to hold live shows with amplified music between 8pm and

11pm. It also removes the need for a licence for unamplified live performances between 8pm and 11pm in all venues.

However, operators will still have to gain an alcohol licence and comply with any restrictions on the performances that are imposed by the Licensing Authority.

Further guidance

- Further information on all aspects of the Licensing Act 2003 is available on the Gov.uk website **www.gov.uk/alcohol-licensing.**

TV and Copyright Licences

KEY FACTS

- If you offer short-stay accommodation (of any kind) to overnight visitors and have installed television sets in the accommodation, you need a 'Hotel and Mobile Units Television Licence' (hotel licence).

- If you play any copyright music in public or on your premises or if it is performed live, you may need a PRS for Music licence.

- If you play recorded music in public on your premises (this includes radio and TVs) you may need a PPL licence.

- If you offer a DVD film library, you need a DVD Concierge licence.

- If you operate an in-room entertainment system you will need a Hotel Vision licence

Television licences

Do I need a special licence?

- **Yes:** if you offer short-stay accommodation to overnight visitors whether in serviced or self-catering accommodation and you provide a device on which your guests can view TV programmes, you need to apply for a 'Hotel and Mobile Units Television Licence' (hotel licence). It should be noted that a licence is required regardless of whether the TV programmes are viewed through a TV, computer, mobile phone, games console, digital box, DVD/VHS recorder or any other device.

Note: despite its name, the hotel licence encompasses accommodation ranging from hotels, guest houses, bed and breakfasts and inns to holiday cottages, flats and chalets through to camping and caravan sites and narrowboats.

The TV Licensing Authority says that you should always take out a hotel licence if you are providing televisions for the use of paying guests. While staying on your property, guests are not covered by their home licence. There is one exception, long-term hotel residents (i.e. those staying over 28 days) are not covered by a hotel licence, but they must have an ordinary television licence.

Note: while accommodation provided in sited caravans falls under the hotel licence scheme, there are different rules for touring caravans or mobile homes. The hirer of a touring caravan or mobile home may be covered by the licence for their home address as long as the television receivers are not being used at their home and caravan or mobile home at the same time.

Hotel licence fees

Your licence fee will be based on the number of units of overnight accommodation you have to let.

- If you have up to 15 units with televisions installed, you will pay one full fee of £145.50
- If you have more than 15 units, you will pay one full fee for the first 15 and an additional £145.50 for every extra 5 units (or fewer).

The hotel licence is available only from TV Licensing. (See *Further Guidance* below for details).

What does it cover?

It will cover any equipment that can be used to watch or record TV programmes in:

- hotels, inns, guest houses, holiday villages, caravans and campsites
- the owner's private rooms on the site
- on-site staff accommodation (if provided by the hotel/accommodation owner)
- lounges or other common rooms that are open to people staying on the site.

It does not cover:

- TV equipment which is not provided by the proprietor of the accommodation
- TV equipment in long-term letting accommodation and for permanent residents.

Note: an important feature of the regulations is that a licence only covers one or more units of guest accommodation 'on the same site' or 'within the same premises'. That means a site or premises that is not divided or separated by any public thoroughfare such as a road or footpath or by another private property. If there is an annex to your premises on the other side of the road from the main building or if you let holiday cottages in different locations, you will need a separate licence for each location.

Copyright licences for music

You will need to obtain copyright licences if you are playing copyright music 'in public' on your premises, whether it is through a radio, TV, CD or DVD player or any other device, or it is performed live.

'In public' means any occasion other than a family/domestic occasion (such as a wedding), and includes guests' rooms. So, even if you have the radio in the breakfast room or simply provide a radio in a guest's room, you may require a licence.

There are two separate licences which relate to recorded music:
- **PRS for Music licence**
  This licence relates to the music itself.
- **PPL licence**
  This licence relates to the recording.

PRS for Music licence

The **Copyright, Designs and Patents Act 1988** states that any use of copyright music in public is possible only with the permission of the person who holds the copyright to each song being played. Of course, such a situation is completely impractical and PRS for Music (formerly the Performing Right Society) has been formed to help you meet your legal obligations. You can apply to them for a single licence rather than having to contact each individual copyright owner – see *Obtaining a licence* below.

Do I need a licence?
- **Yes:** if you play any copyright music in public on your premises.
- **No:** in 2010 the following exemption was introduced for small accommodation businesses:
  1 if you have a B&B or guest house that has *fewer than* four guest bedrooms and
     - the premises is the only holiday accommodation business that you own or operate
     - the premises is also your domestic residence
     - the premises is not licensed for the sale of alcohol
     - facilities are only available to resident guests
  2 if you operate only one self-catering property and that property has fewer than four guest bedrooms.

Is a licence required for copyright music in customers' rooms?
Yes: a licence is required where music can be played in guests' rooms via TVs, radios and other devices.

The PRS for Music Code of Practice clarifies the rights and responsibilities of PRS for Music and businesses that provide music. An ombudsman has also been established to oversee PRS for Music's performance and to adjudicate on complaints.

Obtaining a licence

Further information on obtaining a licence, along with a list of licence tariffs, is available from PRS for Music (see *Further Guidance* below). If a licence is required, PRS for Music has a hotel and restaurant tariff with a separate section for background music in hotel rooms, corridors and foyers via TV or radio (up to 15 rooms with facilities restricted to overnight guests). The current rate (to July 2014) is £47.86 +VAT per 15 bedrooms or part thereof. The full list of tariffs includes other uses of music including:

- the playing of recorded music (i.e. CDs, DVDs or digital files)
- live music
- discos and karaoke machines.

The use of TVs and radios in guests' bedrooms is also covered by these tariffs.

Note: you are required by law to obtain a licence if you need one. If you apply for a licence before you start playing copyright music in a public place, you will be charged a standard rate. If you apply later, or are playing music without a licence, you will be charged a higher rate for the first year of the licence.

Tariffs

PRS for Music licence tariffs vary in accordance with the type of performance (live or recorded), the type of premises, the occasion and the frequency of performances. Holders of a PRS for Music licence will pay the standard royalty rate. For those who have not applied and obtained a licence before the performance, a surcharge of 50% will be applied to the standard rate for the first year. From the second year, all royalties will be charged according to the standard rate.

You can obtain more information by contacting the PRS for Music Customer Service Centre on 0800 068 4828 or by visiting their website: **www.prsformusic.com**.

Tariff for passenger vessels (ocean-going, coastal and inland)

This tariff applies to performances of copyright music within the Society's repertoire on board all vessels including cruise liners and

UPDATED

other ocean or sea-going vessels, and local ferries, lake river and pleasure craft.

These royalty charges apply to royalties due between December 1st and November 30th of the following year.

You can obtain more information and a copy of the PRS for Music code of practice by contacting PRS for Music directly on 0800 068 48 28 or by visiting their website: **www.prsformusic.com**.

Phonographic Performance Limited licences

While PRS for Music licences relate to the copyright in the music itself, there is a separate licence issued by Phonographic Performance Limited (PPL) which relates to the actual recording, whether on a CD, tape, record, or digitally downloaded.

Do I need a PPL licence?
Yes: if you play music in public (this includes the non-residential areas of B&Bs where either customers or staff are allowed) from a record, tape, compact disc, video or digital device, you require a licence (although probably not for activities by charitable bodies).

Probably: if you play music in public from the radio or television (although not usually for activities by not-for-profit bodies).

There are a range of PPL licences with different tariffs. These include licences for:
- the use of sound recordings as background music in foyers, bars and dining rooms
- the use of sound recordings as a featured attraction on the premises (such as dances and discos)
- the use of sound recordings as part of the phone system
- playing music videos.

The cost of the licence varies according to use. The 2014 licence fee for the provision of music in hotel bedrooms is £48.42 per annum per 15 bedrooms. There are separate fees for the provision of music in public areas of the hotel, such as dining rooms and foyers, and a range of discounts related to the size of the premises. Further information on the range of tariffs and discount is available on the PPL website **www.ppluk.com** or by phoning the PPL on 020 7534 1070.

Licences to show DVDs

Do I need a licence?

If you offer films to guests, either through an in-room entertainment system or simply by providing a DVD film library, you need a licence to do so.

Providing films to paying guests without a licence is an infringement of copyright law (the **Copyright, Designs and Patents Act 1988**). It is a civil and, in some cases, criminal offence to show a film in this manner without the permission of the copyright owner (the film studios) or their representatives (the licensing bodies).

A licence permits you to provide DVDs for guests' use, whether guests are using DVD players, lap tops, games consoles or other portable devices. You will be able to hold an unlimited number of DVDs from the represented studios covered by the licence.

Licences are taken out on a different basis depending on the type of guest accommodation:
- bed and breakfast accommodation, guest houses, small hotels and boutique hotels are required to take a licence out on a per room basis
- serviced apartments require one licence per apartment
- chalets and holiday homes require one licence per chalet/home.

Who issues licences?

The main organisations that issue licences to businesses are:
- **Filmbank**: this is a joint venture company owned by Warner Bros. Entertainment and Sony Pictures Releasing. It operates the DVD Concierge Licence scheme and represents many of the leading Hollywood and independent film studios in the area of film usage outside the cinema and home. For more information, visit their website at **www.filmbank.co.uk**
- **The Motion Picture Licensing Company**: www.mplcuk.com which represents more than 400 TV and film producers and distributors. For more information, visit their website at **www.mplcuk.com**.

You may wish to look at these and other companies offering a similar service in order to compare prices. In doing so, make sure that the company you approach represents the studios producing the films you wish to offer customers.

Cost of Filmbank licences

The main form of licence applicable to small accommodation businesses is the DVD Concierge Licence which allows businesses to provide DVDs for their customers' use. There are two forms of this licence:

- annual properties (those open year round) £30 plus VAT per room/unit
- seasonal properties (open for eight months or less) £20 plus VAT per room/unit.

The fees payable are for the licence only and accommodation providers would continue to purchase DVDs as usual. The licence fees quoted for guest accommodation apply when no extra charge for the DVD is made to the guest. If a charge is levied, as in most hotels, then a higher licence fee applies.

Avoiding DVD licences
Smaller businesses may choose to avoid the purchase of a licence by removing DVDs. A licence is not required if guests bring their own DVDs to watch.

Further guidance

- More information on TV licensing for accommodation businesses is available on the TV licensing website
  www.tvlicensing.co.uk
- PRS for Music Customer Service Centre, tel: 0800 068 4828
  www.prsformusic.com
- Phonographic Performance Limited licences: contact the PPL information line: 020 7534 1070
  www.ppluk.com
- Filmbank 020 7984 5965 or email
  dvdconcierge@filmbank.co.uk
  You can also find out more on the Filmbank website
  www.filmbank.co.uk
- The Motion Picture Licensing Company, tel: 01323 649 647, email: **ukinfo@mplc.com**
  or visit their website **www.mplcuk.com**

LICENCES & CONSENTS

MARKETING

GUESTS

FOOD & DRINK

HEALTH & SAFETY

STAFF

BUSINESS MANAGEMENT & TAX

FURTHER INFORMATION

Planning and Building

KEY FACTS

- Planning permission and building regulations apply if you are considering starting a business offering serviced or self-catering accommodation, or if you plan to convert, extend or make structural alterations to an existing property or construct a new building.
- Contact the planning department of your local authority for advice on planning permission.
- Asbestos can be found in buildings and can pose a serious health risk. You must identify whether the building contains asbestos, keep an up-to-date record of the location and condition of asbestos-containing materials, assess any risk, and prepare a plan to manage that risk.

Essential first steps

Planning permission and building regulations are the essential first steps if you are considering offering serviced or self-catering accommodation. Serviced accommodation includes:
- hotels
- guest houses
- bed and breakfasts
- farmhouses
- inns.

Planning permission

You should contact the planning department of your local authority for advice on planning permission at a very early stage if you are considering:
- starting a new business
- converting or extending your premises.

Planning policies on providing tourism businesses, especially visitor accommodation, will be set out in the authority's Local Development Framework.

'Change of use'

Even if you only wish to start offering a simple bed and breakfast in your home or to equip an existing building as a holiday cottage where no structural alterations to the property will be carried out, you may need 'change of use' planning permission to do so.

Change of use consent

There is sometimes confusion about whether converting a property from a residential dwelling to a bed and breakfast establishment requires the owner to gain change of use approval. This confusion stems from two sources – the first being that there are no hard and fast rules as to what constitutes change of use and the second from the fact that there are two change of use requirements:

- the first is related to planning permission
- the second is related to building regulations.

Planning permission

In planning terms, consent from the council must be gained if there is any 'material change' of use to a property or building. In most cases it is relatively straightforward as to what constitutes a material change of use (e.g. converting a house into a commercial building or a block of flats).

However, there is a grey area as to how much change is allowed before that change materially affects the purpose for which the building is used. That is, at what point does a residential house become principally a premises offering accommodation for visitors? This issue is particularly relevant for bed and breakfast properties where the property is simultaneously a residential property and a commercial property.

To clarify this area, local authorities have developed a range of measures to determine whether a material change of use has occurred and planning consent is required. These rules generally relate to the proportion of the property that has been given over to the B&B business, which can be determined in a number of ways, the most usual relating to:

- the number of bedrooms as a proportion of the total number of bedrooms on the property, or
- the area of the building used for the B&B as a proportion of the total building.

However, some local authorities use the 'six-bed rule', i.e. consent for change of use must be sought where the business provides six or more bedspaces (not to be confused with bedrooms) for customers.

If you are considering operating a B&B, you should consult with the local authority planning officers to determine whether change of use consent is required. Even if you have previously operated a similar B&B in another destination where no consent was required, you should contact the council as their interpretation of a material change to the use of a property could be different.

Building regulations

The second change of use requirement is under the **Building Regulations 2000**.

Under the Building Regulations, there is a material change of use where there is a change in the purposes for which, or the circumstances in which, a building is used, so that after the change 'the building is used as an hotel or a boarding house, where previously it was not'. As with determining whether planning consent is required, different local authorities have different guidelines as to whether a property is deemed to be a hotel or boarding house under these regulations. Potential B&B operators should check with their local authority to determine whether change of use consent is required.

You should also note that the Building Regulations' definition of 'material change of use' differs substantially from the meaning of 'material change of use' in the **Town and Country Planning Act 1990**, which has given rise to a great deal of litigation. Planning permission may be required for a change of use where Building Regulation approval is not needed and vice versa.

If consent is required, you must make an application using the 'Full Plans' application process, as domestic buildings that are not exclusively used as private dwellings (e.g. holiday accommodation and dwellings providing bed and breakfast) are subject to the **Regulatory Reform (Fire Safety) Order 2005**.

Note: even if planning consent is not required, you may still require building regulations consent. You may also require building regulations consent even if you are not contemplating any structural changes in turning your house into a bed and breakfast establishment.

Granting planning permission

Local authorities' policies on granting planning permission vary and any proposal will be checked against these policies. In deciding whether or not to grant planning permission, where it is needed, the council will take into account the effects on neighbours and the environment, the loss of residential accommodation, traffic generation, access from the highway, car parking facilities and the number of bedrooms offered for letting.

Restrictions on what you can do are usually stricter in specially protected areas such as:
- National Parks
- Green Belts
- Conservation Areas
- Areas of Outstanding Natural Beauty (AONB).

Note: you may also need consent for any signage for your property (see the *Signs for your Premises* section).

Building regulations

Building Regulations apply whenever a building is erected, extended, materially altered or made subject to a material change of use. They also cover other works and fittings such as:
- new drainage and sanitary installations
- new heating installations
- structural alterations to a building
- alterations which have an effect on existing means of escape from fire
- replacement windows and external doors in dwellings
- electrical installations in dwellings
- change to a building's energy status and renovation or replacement of thermal elements of a building (such as re-roofing, replacement cladding, re-plastering, dry lining, external render, and renovation or replacement of existing floors).

Note: even if you are not thinking of altering your house to accommodate bed and breakfast guests, and planning permission is not required, you may still be required to do work to your property in order to meet building regulations requirements. Again, you need to contact the building control department of your local authority as early as possible.

Energy Performance Certificates

All properties that are newly built, sold or rented are required to have an Energy Performance Certificate (EPC). These certificates provide information on a building's energy use and carbon dioxide emissions and are accompanied by a report with suggestions on how to reduce them. A Certificate is valid for 10 years, after which it must be renewed.

A building's EPC must be provided to any person who wishes to purchase or rent the building. However, an EPC is not required where a property is:

- rented out for less than a cumulative period of four months within a 12 month period, or
- rented out through a licensing arrangement whereby the holiday-maker does not have exclusive use of the property during the period of their booking.

This means that self-catering properties are not required to gain and provide EPCs for customers, provided that the agreement under which the property is let is a 'licence to occupy'. A licence to occupy is the type of agreement that hotels have with customers, whereby staff can enter the property to undertake essential work, rather than a tenancy agreement whereby the landlord must gain the permission of the tenant to enter the property.

Managing asbestos

Regulations governing the management of asbestos in non-domestic properties are the **Control of Asbestos Regulations 2012**.

Many buildings throughout the country contain asbestos, which can pose a serious health risk if not managed properly.

The legal duty relates to its management, not necessarily its removal. The regulations require you to:

- identify whether the building contains asbestos
- keep an up-to-date record of the location and condition of asbestos-containing materials
- assess the risk and prepare a plan to manage that risk.

The guestrooms and all common parts (e.g. corridors/dining room) of your property will be considered to be non-domestic and therefore subject to the regulations. Any private areas used only by the owner of the accommodation will be considered to be domestic and therefore not subject to the regulations. This applies to both serviced and self-catering accommodation.

If you think that your property contains asbestos, seek advice from an expert. Asbestos is only dangerous when disturbed: if it is safely managed and contained it does not present a health risk.

LICENCES & CONSENTS

MARKETING

GUESTS

FOOD & DRINK

HEALTH & SAFETY

STAFF

BUSINESS MANAGEMENT & TAX

FURTHER INFORMATION

Further guidance

- Information and advice on whether you need planning permission is available from the Planning Department of your local authority
- Planning Portal, the Government's online service for planning, offers free guidance on all aspects of planning **www.planningportal.gov.uk**
- For further information and guidance on asbestos:
  - contact the Planning and Building Control Department or the Environmental Health Department in your local authority
  - contact the Health and Safety Executive **www.hse.gov.uk/asbestos**
  - INDG223: *A Short Guide to Managing Asbestos in Premises* can be downloaded from the HSE website.

LICENCES & CONSENTS

MARKETING

GUESTS

FOOD & DRINK

HEALTH & SAFETY

STAFF

BUSINESS MANAGEMENT & TAX

FURTHER INFORMATION

Signs for Your Premises

KEY FACTS

- If you display any outdoor signs and/or advertisements you may need to apply to the planning authority for consent to display the proposed sign.

- The need for consent from the planning authority depends on whether signs are fully, partially or non-illuminated and where they are situated.

- You will also need to ensure that any signs displayed are not misleading, as this could constitute a breach of unfair trading and misleading marketing legislation.

- The highways department of your local authority can advise on white on brown tourism signs.

Background

Do the Regulations apply to me?

Yes: if you display any outdoor signs and/or advertisements, you need to comply with:

- **Town and Country Planning (Control of Advertisements) Regulations 2007**
- **The Consumer Protection Regulations 2008** (CPRs) relating to unfair trading and misleading marketing (see *Unfair Trading Practices* section).

Planning regulations and permission

The display of all outdoor signs and advertisements is controlled by local planning authorities under the provisions of **Town and Country Planning (Control of Advertisements) Regulations 2007**.

Local planning authorities are required to exercise their powers under the Regulations with regard to amenity and public safety, taking into account relevant development plan policies in so far as they relate to amenity (including both visual and aural amenity) and public safety, as well as any other relevant factors.

These regulations can be complex and you are strongly advised to seek the advice of the planning department of your local authority (see *Further guidance* below) before commissioning and setting up any signs for your premises. A very brief summary of the regulations is given here.

- 'Express consent' means that you have to apply to the planning authority for consent to display the proposed sign.
- 'Deemed consent' means that consent is deemed to have been given by the planning authority and that you do not have to apply for it.

Signs on your premises

Illuminated and non-illuminated signs

- **Fully illuminated signs** always require express consent from the planning authority (although this is not normally the case if the sign is displayed inside a window, rather than on the wall or doorway outside).
- **Partially illuminated signs** (e.g. where letters only, and not the background, are illuminated) may not require express consent.
- **Non-illuminated signs** can normally be displayed with deemed consent if they are fixed to the building, although there are limitations placed on the height of the sign and on the size of any characters or symbols on it.

Listed Buildings
If your property is a Listed Building, you will always have to obtain Listed Building consent before you put up a sign.

Signs at the entrance to your premises
You may normally put a non-illuminated sign by your gate, driveway or within the grounds of your establishment with deemed consent (subject to limitations on overall size, height and size of characters or symbols).

Signs in advance of your premises
If you wish to put up directional signs by the side of the roads approaching your establishment, e.g. in a field overlooking the road (with the landowner's permission, of course), you must always seek the express consent of the planning authority.

Flags
Provided that your premises are not within areas of special control or other areas with protective designations, flag advertisements that do not require express consent are restricted to:

- a single flag from a single flagpole projecting from the premises with either the company name or logo of the company or the advertising of a specific event of limited duration, such as a sale
- two flags on flagstaffs not attached to a building.

Special controls

In sensitive places, e.g. Conservation Areas, the deemed consent may be removed by an Article 4 Declaration. You will have to apply for consent for signs on or at the entrance to your premises. In some rural localities an Area of Special Control Advertisements may restrict all outdoor advertising.

Ensuring signs are not misleading

You should also ensure that any signs displayed are not misleading. For example, it is illegal to display a quality sign (from VisitEngland or the AA) on a non-assessed property or to display a sign showing an incorrect star rating.

For more information on misleading signs, see the *Unfair Trading Practices* section.

White-on-brown tourism signs

Hotels, guest houses and bed and breakfasts can apply for these signs but, in practice, accommodation establishments have been less successful with their applications than visitor attractions.

The first step is to contact the highways department of your local authority who will advise you about procedures, local policy and the cost of such signs. Each local highways authority will have its own guidelines that balance local environmental and road safety interests with those of the tourism industry..

Your local highway authority controls signs on the local roads in its area and sets local policy on brown signs. The Highways Agency (HA) controls signs on trunk roads and motorways.

Following a joint review by the Department for Transport (DfT) and HA, a new standard was issued in February 2004 for tourist signing on the trunk road network and new guidance was issued for the local roads in England. These are available on the Highways Agency website.

Note: The Government has undertaken a review of all signage on the roads network, including white-on-brown signs. As part of this process the guidance has been modified to ensure that priority is given to genuine tourist attractions rather than wider retail, sport or leisure facilities. There has also been a move towards greater transparency in the application process and improving processing times. While this guidance only applies to motorways and trunk roads, local Highway Authorities will be encouraged to apply similar standards.

Further guidance

- For informal advice or to apply for consent, contact the planning department of your local authority.
- The publication *Outdoor Advertisements and Signs – A Guide for Advertisers* can be downloaded from the Department for Communities and Local Government website **www.gov.uk**
- The Highways Agency website contains a range of guidance publications related to tourism signage on both trunk and non-trunk roads on a dedicated page on their website **www.highways.gov.uk/our-road-network/tourist-signs**
- Your local tourist board or your local authority may also be able to advise you on the local situation with white-on-brown signs.

LICENCES & CONSENTS MARKETING GUESTS FOOD & DRINK HEALTH & SAFETY STAFF BUSINESS MANAGEMENT & TAX FURTHER INFORMATION

UPDATED

Unfair Trading Practices

KEY FACTS

- Businesses have a general duty not to undertake unfair trading practices – the relevant legislation is the Consumer Protection from Unfair Trading Regulations (CPRs).

- The CPRs aid in determining whether certain advertising and marketing practices are misleading, aggressive or lack due diligence.

- In addition to this general duty, there are 31 business practices that are banned outright, such as displaying a quality mark without authorisation.

- The Business Protection Regulations impose further restrictions on how companies compare their products to rival products from other companies.

Background

The **Consumer Protection from Unfair Trading Regulations 2008** (Consumer Protection Regulations) implement the EU's Unfair Commercial Practices Directive (UCPD). The UCPD aims to harmonise European legislation preventing business practices that are unfair to consumers.

The aim of the legislation is to make it easier for traders in one Member State to market and sell their products to consumers in other Member States. This is particularly relevant to the tourism sector.

The **Business Protection from Misleading Marketing Regulations 2008** (Business Protection Regulations) also implement the EU's Unfair Commercial Practices Directive. These regulations tighten restrictions relating to how companies compare their products to rival products from other companies.

Do the Regulations apply to me?
Yes: if you are either:
- advertising your accommodation facilities using any form of

media (including online and via social media)
- making statements about your facilities to the public.

Unfair trading

What constitutes an unfair trading practice?

The aim of the CPRs is to provide a framework for determining whether certain practices are misleading, aggressive or lack due diligence on the basis that they would alter the behaviour of the average customer. In other words, if it can be determined that the customer made a purchase that they otherwise would not have done had they known the full facts of the matter, then the business has engaged in unfair practices.

This covers engaging in misleading practices such as making false or deceptive statements in marketing material or omitting important information that would have a bearing on the customer's purchasing decision.

Accommodation examples

Examples relating to accommodation facilities could include statements made about:
- the quality of the accommodation (see also *Practices banned outright* below)
- the amenities
- the location of the accommodation premises
- services related to the accommodation.

For example, it would be a false statement if you advertised that your accommodation was 'five minutes from the beach', when it actually is a half-hour drive, or that 'the rooms are spacious with panoramic views' if this only applies to one room.

Similarly, if you omitted to notify customers of the cost of making calls from their room or that you were undertaking refurbishment work that either closed facilities or generated considerable noise or dust, this could be deemed to be misleading.

Practices banned outright

While much of what constitutes an unfair practice will have to be determined through case law, the new legislation lists 31 practices that are to be banned outright. These practices include:
- displaying a quality mark (such as the accommodation grading scheme mark) without having the necessary authorisation. This includes displaying a quality mark that is out-of-date
- falsely claiming that a premise or product has been

LICENCES & CONSENTS

MARKETING

GUESTS

FOOD & DRINK

HEALTH & SAFETY

STAFF

BUSINESS MANAGEMENT & TAX

FURTHER INFORMATION

approved or endorsed by a public body such as VisitEngland
- falsely stating that an offer will only be available for a limited time.

So, if you were to display on your premises an incorrect VisitEngland Quality Rose star rating, or an outdated tourist board rating such as a Crown or Diamond classification and grading, this would be regarded as a breach of the regulations.

Unfair comparison

In addition to the Consumer Protection Regulations, the **Business Protection from Misleading Marketing Regulations 2008** tighten the legislation relating to comparison marketing. These regulations specify that companies must not use advertising to:
- compare products or materials that are not designed for the same purpose
- confuse people as to the advertiser and the competitor
- present imitations or replicas of products bearing a protected trade mark or trade name
- take unfair advantage of the reputation of competitors' trademarks, trade names, other distinguishing marks, or country of origin information.

Accommodation examples

Examples relating to accommodation facilities could include:
- taking out an advertisement that unfavourably compares the cost of staying at a neighbouring hotel with staying at your hotel would be deemed to be unfair if you failed to mention that the neighbouring hotel was a five star property while yours was a three star property
- describing your guest house as "the Torquay Hilton", even if you consider this to be a tongue-in-cheek description.

Enforcement and penalties

Your local trading standards office is responsible for enforcing the Regulations.

Anyone who breaches the Regulations can be prosecuted for a criminal offence by a local trading standards office and subject to a fine and/or, in extreme cases, a prison sentence of up to two years. In addition, it could lead to a civil claim – see *Misrepresentation* over page.

Defence against a charge of Unfair Trading

Possible defences against a charge of unfair trading include:
- you made a pure mistake and were not given the opportunity to remedy the situation

- your statement was based on information supplied by a third party
- the statement was made by some 'other person' ('other person' does not mean any of your employees).

However, in any defence, you would still have to show that you took all reasonable care and exercised all due diligence to check that the facts were true in any publication or statement. You should keep written records of those efforts so you can prove what action you took (e.g. a copy of your brochure or information sheet marked to show the checks you made).

Misrepresentation

Engaging in unfair trading practices can not only result in a criminal prosecution (see *Enforcement and penalties* above) but it may also result in a civil claim being brought against you by any person who has suffered loss as a result of a false statement. This stems from what is referred to in law as misrepresentation.

When misrepresentation occurs

Misrepresentation occurs where a party is induced to enter into a contract by certain statements that later turn out to be untrue. With respect to accommodation premises, these could again include misleading statements about the accommodation's:

- quality
- amenities
- location.

For example, if Mr Anderson and his family had booked into a bed and breakfast with an assurance that it was only 'five minutes from the beach' and it turned out to be a half-hour drive he would be able to either:

- refuse to continue with the booking and claim damages from you for any losses incurred as a result
- continue staying with you but claim damages for his and his family's distress and disappointment.

Other considerations

For any promotional material, you should bear in mind the following.

- **Advertising codes** (for broadcast and non-broadcast media) are issued by the Committee of Advertising Practice (CAP) and require advertisements and sales promotions to be legal, decent, honest and truthful. Advertising codes also deal with specific issues, including the availability of products at the advertised price and VAT inclusion in prices.

LICENCES & CONSENTS

MARKETING

GUESTS

FOOD & DRINK

HEALTH & SAFETY

STAFF

BUSINESS MANAGEMENT & TAX

FURTHER INFORMATION

- The requirements of the **Package Travel, Package Holidays and Package Tours Regulations 1992** – see the *Holiday Packages* for more information.

Social Media

Many operators advertise and market their business through social media – for example, having a Facebook account for the business and/or a Twitter feed attached to their website.

It is important to realise that while you may use a far more relaxed or 'chatty' style of communication when using social media than you would in print or on your main website, everything that you post via social media must still comply with all aspects of the CPRs. It is therefore essential to re-read anything that you are about to post using social media to make sure that it is accurate, is not open to misinterpretation and does not make unfair comparisons.

Further guidance

- Your local trading standards office is responsible for enforcing the Regulations and should be able to give you further guidance.
- Copies of a guidance publication on the regulations *The Consumer Protection from Unfair Trading Regulations: a basic guide for business* can be downloaded from the Office for Fair Trading (OFT) website **www.oft.gov.uk**
- Further information on the advertising codes can be obtained from the Committee of Advertising Practice (CAP) website **www.cap.org.uk**

Direct Marketing

KEY FACTS

- If you make direct marketing calls to individuals, or send direct marketing faxes to individuals or businesses, you are required to comply with direct marketing legislation.

- As a business, you are not allowed to make direct marketing calls to individuals who have declined to receive such calls or who have registered with the Telephone Preference Service (TPS).

- If you send e-mail and/or text/picture/video marketing messages to advertise your business, the **Privacy and Electronic Communications (EC Directive) Regulations 2003** apply.

- The **Consumer Contracts (Information, Cancellation and Additional Charges) Regulations 2013** came into force in June 2014, replacing the **Consumer Protection (Distance Selling) Regulations**. These regulations apply to goods and services sold over the internet, by phone or by mail order. However, they **do not apply to contracts to provide accommodation, transport, catering or leisure services**.

Direct marketing by telephone or electronic mail

Privacy and Electronic Communications (EC Directive) Regulations 2003 were introduced to protect individuals, and in some cases businesses, against receiving direct marketing material by phone or electronic media (e.g. internet or text messaging) without their prior approval.

The regulations are overseen and enforced by the Information Commissioner's Office **www.ico.gov.uk**. This is an independent authority established by the Government.

Do the Regulations apply to me?
- **Yes:** if you make direct marketing calls, emails, texts or other electronic communications to individuals or businesses, including the use of cookies on your website.

What do the Regulations cover?

Direct marketing phone calls

As a business, you are not allowed to make a direct marketing call to any individual (including sole traders and, except in Scotland, partnerships), if they have told you that they do not want to receive such calls **or** they have registered with the Telephone Preference Service (TPS).

Direct marketing faxes

As a business, you are not allowed to send a direct marketing fax to anyone, whether a consumer or a business, if the recipient has registered with the Fax Preference Service (FPS). In addition, you must not send a direct marketing fax to an individual who has not previously consented to receive it.

> **Note:** the TPS and FPS are services set up by the Direct Marketing Association (DMA). They maintain registers of all those who have stated that they do not want to receive direct marketing calls or faxes.

Emails and text messaging

The Regulations define electronic mail as "any text, voice, sound, or image message sent over a public electronic communications network" and includes messages sent via social media.

The regulations require you to obtain individuals' prior consent before sending unsolicited direct marketing via e-mail or text messages. When undertaking any marketing you must also identify your business and provide valid address to which the recipient can send an opt-out request.

The soft opt-in

There is an exception to the need to gain prior consent which is called the "soft opt-in". This allows you to call or send electronic mail for marketing purposes to individuals where you obtained their contact details in the course of a sale or negotiations for the sale of a product or service in the past (i.e. previous customers).

For the soft opt-in to apply, the individual must have been provided with a simple means of refusing the use of their contact details at the time they were initially collected (e.g. a tick-box on a paper or on-line booking form) and the material you send them must relate to similar products and services only (i.e. you cannot send them advertising material for someone else's business).

The material you send must also provide the opportunity for the person to opt-out of any subsequent communications.

How do I comply, and what are the costs?

If you intend to make any 'cold' direct marketing calls (calls where permission has not been given to do so beforehand) to individuals or send faxes to individuals or businesses, you need to check the numbers first against the TPS or FPS registers, as appropriate. If you make regular cold calls, you need to check the numbers every 28 days.

The cost of access to the TPS register varies, depending on the type and level of access you require. In order to ensure that you have the most appropriate package, call the TPS/FPS information pack line (see *Further Guidance* below). There is also useful information on the TPS website **www.tpsonline.org.uk**. If you use a telemarketing company to run a telephone campaign for you, you do not need to subscribe.

Using Premium Rate Numbers

Premium rate numbers generally begin with 09, 118, 0871, 0872 and 0873. Mobile text shortcode numbers – the five- and six-digit numbers that you can use to enter text competitions, give to charity via your mobile, download mobile games, etc. – are also considered premium rate. The 0870 and 0845 numbers are not affected.

Premium Rate Numbers are currently regulated by PhonePayPlus **www.phonepayplus.org.uk** under an Ofcom approved code of practice.

- **Pricing:** pricing information is to be clearly written wherever you display the number of the media (eg. it applies to electronic, website and print information).
- **Undue delay:** there should not be an unfair delay before a caller can access the service required. Callers must be informed of the expected time it will take to have their call answered and, if applicable, of their position in any queuing system..
- **Prior permission licenses:** some services require prior permission from PhonepayPlus before they can operate on a premium-rate line – such as international dial-through services for example. A list of those services exempt from prior permission can be found on the PhonepayPlus website.
- **Customer care contact number:** a number must be provided for customers with complaints or concerns to call. This number can be the same or an alternative 087 number.

The use of 'cookies' on websites

A 'cookie' is a piece of data stored by a website within a browser, and then subsequently sent back to the same website by the browser. Typically, a cookie remembers a user's preferences or settings when they revisit the website. More recently, businesses

LICENCES & CONSENTS

MARKETING

GUESTS

FOOD & DRINK

HEALTH & SAFETY

STAFF

BUSINESS MANAGEMENT & TAX

FURTHER INFORMATION

have introduced 'tracking cookies' as a way to compile long-term records of individual's browsing histories so that products and offers can be targeted to specific customers or so a picture can be developed of a customer's buying patterns.

You are not allowed to use cookies or similar devices unless:
- customers are provided with clear and comprehensive information about the purposes of the storage of, or access to, that information, and;
- have given their consent.

The Regulations are not prescriptive about the sort of information that you should provide but the text should be sufficiently comprehensive and intelligible to allow customers to clearly understand the potential consequences of allowing storage and access to the information collected by the cookie should they wish to do so.

Guidance on the use of cookies and other similar devices is provided on the Information Commissioner's Office website **www.ico.gov.uk**. The ICO also produces a guidance publication, *Guidance on the rules on use of cookies and similar technologies*, which can be downloaded from the website.

Direct marketing by electronic mail

If you send e-mail and text/picture/video marketing messages to advertise your business then you must comply with the **Privacy and Electronic Communications (EC Directive) Regulations 2003**.

The Information Commissioner is responsible for enforcing the regulations.

What do the Regulations require?
Under the 2003 Regulations you are not allowed, by law, to send unsolicited marketing material by e-mail to an individual subscriber without previous consent nor send any marketing material by e-mail (whether solicited or unsolicited) to any subscriber without revealing your full identify or a valid address to which the recipient can send an opt-out request.

You may e-mail marketing material to previous guests at your establishment, providing the recipients have a simple means of refusing the use of their contact details for marketing purposes at the time their details were collected or at the time of each subsequent communication (this should be free of charge except for the cost of transmission). This is known as the 'soft opt in' criteria.

UPDATED

You are not obliged to check against the TPS register because you should already have established prior consent or satisfied the soft opt in criteria before your transmission.

Note: If you intend to take bookings over the Internet refer to the Electronic (EC Directive) Regulations 2002. These can be found on the BIS website **www.bis.gov.uk/files/file14635.pdf**.

Distance selling

In June 2014 the **Consumer Contracts (Information, Cancellation and Additional Charges) Regulations 2013** came into force, replacing the **Consumer Protection (Distance Selling) Regulations 2000** and the **Consumer Protection (Distance Selling) (Amendment) Regulations 2005**. For small accommodation businesses, the new legislation does not provide any significant changes to the existing legislation.

These Regulations apply to goods and services that are not sold in 'face-to-face' transactions. That is items sold over the internet, by phone or by mail order where the customer is not able to inspect the goods and services that they are purchasing.

The purpose of these Regulations is to provide additional rights to consumers buying at a distance, to encourage confidence in this method of transaction. The information that must be provided in these transactions includes details about:

- the business
- the goods or services you are selling
- payment arrangements
- delivery arrangements
- consumers' right to cancel their orders.

The Regulations also require the business to provide those goods or services within 30 days.

Note: however, it is important to note that the Regulations do not apply to contracts to provide accommodation, transport, catering and leisure services where the contract provides for a specific date or period of performance (e.g. a concert or sports event that is only being staged on specific dates).

It should also be noted that the Regulations do not apply to goods and services sold to other businesses (these are business-to-business contracts) and only apply to transactions that are normally

LICENCES & CONSENTS

UPDATED

MARKETING

GUESTS

FOOD & DRINK

HEALTH & SAFETY

STAFF

BUSINESS MANAGEMENT & TAX

FURTHER INFORMATION

undertaken at distance and where there are systems in place for trading in this way.

So even if you occasionally sell products and services other than the services listed as exempt above, the Regulations only apply if this is your normal way of selling these products and services.

Further guidance

- TPS registration line: 0845 0700 707 (consumer line). **www.tpsonline.org.uk**
- FPS registration line: 0845 0700 702 (consumer line). **www.fpsonline.org.uk**
- The Direct Marketing Association runs the TPS, FPS and other preference services and provides further information on its website, **www.dma.org.uk**
- Guidance on the **Privacy and Electronic Communications (EC Directive) Regulations 2003** is available at **www.bis.gov.uk/files/file14635.pdf**
- Guidance on **Consumer Contracts (Information, Cancellation and Additional Charges) Regulations 2013** is available on **www.gov.uk/government/uploads/system/uploads/attachment_data/file/310044/bis-13-1368-consumer-contracts-information-cancellation-and-additional-payments-regulations-guidance.pdf**.

Holiday Packages

KEY FACTS

- If you offer a package of services that lasts at least 24 hours and includes at least two out of three of transport, accommodation and other significant visitor services, then you are probably subject to the Package Holiday Regulations.
- The Package Holiday Regulations include provisions relating to the marketing, booking and delivery of the package.

Package Holiday Regulations

The **Package Travel, Package Holidays and Package Tours Regulations 1992** (amended in 1995) affect many accommodation providers.

These Regulations concern the marketing, sale and performance of package holidays. They apply not only to the big companies offering overseas package holidays, but also those offering domestic packages, including hotels offering inclusive holidays and breaks (for example, weekend theme breaks such as murder mystery weekends or golfing breaks).

Enforcement and penalties

There are criminal penalties for non-compliance. Trading Standards are responsible for enforcing the legislation.

Do the Regulations apply to me?

Yes: if you are offering a package of services for sale at an inclusive price that includes at least two of the services listed below and the package lasts for at least 24 hours or includes overnight accommodation, you will probably be offering a 'package' that is subject to the Regulations:

- transport
- accommodation
- other visitor services that are a significant part of the package and not ancillary to transport or accommodation (e.g. excursions, access to a golf course, theatre tickets,

but not educational, business or conference services).

What do the Regulations require?

The Regulations contain provisions relating to the marketing, booking and delivery of the package including:

- information:
  - to be included in the brochure
  - to be provided before the booking is made and
  - to be provided in good time
- the contents and form of the booking
- arrangements for transfers of bookings, cancellations, price revisions and other significant changes to the arrangements
- liability for not providing the services agreed
- security of guests' monies in the event of the insolvency of your business, e.g. bonding, insurance and holding monies in trust.

Government guidance on what is a package

The Department for Business, Innovation and Skills (BIS) provides guidance for tourism businesses on the application of the Package Holiday Regulations.

The guidance provides a good explanation as to when services you are supplying are considered to be a package and when they are not. It also addresses the tricky issue of 'dynamic packaging', where the customer builds their own package from a list of products and services that the operator provides. In simple terms, this is considered a package when:

- the aggregated cost of the components chosen by the customer is different from the cost of the separate components (i.e. a discount is provided if customers book accommodation and another service)
- the cost to the customer is not disaggregated when they choose the different components (i.e. an 'all-in' price is provided rather than a sum of the parts).

A copy of the guidance is available at **www.gov.uk/government/ publications/the-package-travel-regulations-question-and-answer-guidance-for-organisers-and-retailers**. Although the guidance offers a good assessment of what constitutes a package, you are advised to seek specific advice about your own holiday products as this remains a complex area.

Note: the European Commission is currently revising the Package Travel Directive to try to ensure that it is better suited to dealing with dynamic packaging and how tourism products and services are sold over the internet. This may result in the development of legislation that affects how you advertise third party products and services on your website (e.g. links to local attractions or facilities).

Further guidance

Further information on the requirements of the Package Travel Regulations is available from your local Trading Standards office.

LICENCES & CONSENTS

MARKETING

GUESTS

FOOD & DRINK

HEALTH & SAFETY

STAFF

BUSINESS MANAGEMENT & TAX

FURTHER INFORMATION

LICENCES & CONSENTS

MARKETING

GUESTS

FOOD & DRINK

HEALTH & SAFETY

STAFF

BUSINESS MANAGEMENT & TAX

FURTHER INFORMATION

GUESTS

Bookings

KEY FACTS

- Once you have accepted a booking from a guest, you normally have to honour the booking.
- All accommodation providers should abide by good practice with regard to booking procedures.

Booking contract

Once you have accepted a booking from a guest, you normally have to honour the booking (see the *Accepting Guests* section for circumstances where a booking does not have to be honoured). This is because once you have agreed the terms of the booking with a guest (e.g. the dates, accommodation type and price) and then accepted the booking, a legally enforceable contract exists between you and the guest.

This applies equally whether the arrangement has been made verbally over the telephone, by fax, by e-mail or in writing. You may change the terms of the booking at a later date, provided that both you and the guest agree to the change of terms.

To avoid any problems with cancellations, no-shows or curtailment (when a guest cuts their stay short), you are strongly recommended to have a cancellation policy. For the cancellation procedure to be enforceable, you must make it clear to guests before accepting a booking. See *Cancellations and No-shows* for further details.

Booking terms and conditions

Larger hotels and letting agencies may have arranged for their lawyers to prepare full booking conditions, and any operator that needs to comply with the Package Travel Regulations will require them. However, it is recommended that all operators have a policy relating to deposits or cancellations.

If you have any special arrangements like these, you must give guests the full details before they book to ensure the arrangements are part of the booking contract and binding on the guest.

In developing any terms and conditions for the provision of goods and services to customers, there are three important points to keep in mind.

1 Regardless of your terms and conditions, the law requires you to use reasonable skill and care in providing the underlying services.

2 You can't contract yourself out of your legal responsibilities. For example, you cannot have a condition which states you are not responsible for any injury a guest may sustain when the Health and Safety Act says you have a responsibility towards your guests. Similarly, you cannot say that you will only deal with complaints that are brought to your attention while the guest is staying in your property.

3 The law does not allow you to limit your liability to a guest for death or personal injury arising out of your negligence, or that of an employee or agent. In respect of any other loss or damage, you can only restrict your liability towards a guest as far as is reasonable.

See also the *Cancellations and No-shows* section for more information.

Good practice

As a matter of good practice, you should keep a clear, accurate record of the arrangements for each of your bookings. You might also want to have a simple checklist by the telephone or computer, to remind you of the details you need to run through with each guest, e.g.:

- pricing
- deposit
- cancellations
- data protection.

Although, ideally, you should confirm all bookings in writing to the guest, this may not be practical. However, you are advised to confirm in writing the booking details for any longer stays, larger groups or bookings that are more complex than usual.

Further guidance

Booking contracts and conditions are a complex area of law. For any detailed information or assistance, you should seek professional legal advice.

Registration and Data Protection

KEY FACTS

- All serviced and self-catering accommodation premises must keep a record of all guests over the age of 16. The record should include their full name and nationality.
- You must keep each guest's details for at least 12 months.
- If you hold any personal information on guests or any other individuals, including employees (other than on odd scraps of paper), the **Data Protection Act** applies.

Keeping a register of your guests

Does this apply to me?
- **Yes:** all serviced and self-catering accommodation premises must keep a record of all guests over the age of 16 (**Immigration (Hotel Records) Order 1972 (as amended)**).

Note: the 1972 Order above is considered to be obsolete and is being considered for repeal as part of the Government's Red Tape Challenge. However, while it is still on the books, it remains a legal requirement.

What do I need to record?
To comply with the **Immigration (Hotel Records) Order 1972** you need to collect the following information from each guest on their arrival:
- full name
- nationality

For all who are not British, Irish or Commonwealth guests, on arrival:
- passport number and place of issue (or other document which shows their identity and nationality).

(you are not legally required to take a guest's home address or contact number)

For all who are not British, Irish or Commonwealth guests, on/before departure:
- details of their next destination (including the address, if known).

Note: diplomats and their family and staff do not have to register.

What about the format of the register?

There is no set format for the register. It could be a visitors' book or an exercise book, but you must keep each guest's details for at least 12 months and have the register available for inspection by a police officer or duly authorised person at all times.

It may be, of course, that you are given the necessary details at the time of booking, but you should check them when the guests arrive and make sure that you have all the information you are required to collect. Even if your local police have traditionally shown no interest in these records, circumstances could change.

Data protection

The holding and use of personal information on individuals is regulated by the **Data Protection Act 1998**. As the provisions in the Act are extensive, you should read the paragraphs below to see if they apply to you.

Note: the paragraphs in this section focus on personal data held on guests, as this is perhaps the most relevant situation for smaller accommodation businesses. However, the Act does apply equally to personal data held on other individuals, including employees, although the specific provisions vary. For further information, contact the Information Commissioner's Office.

What is the purpose of the Act?

The Act is to protect the privacy of individuals (data subjects) by preventing the misuse or unauthorised use of personal information (personal data) that is held by others (data controllers). The Act achieves this by:
- regulating the use of personal data held by data controllers, and
- giving rights to data subjects.

Does this Act apply to me?

- **Yes:** if you hold any personal information on guests or any other individuals (including employees, but not organisations) on a computer, any automated system or in a manual filing system (including index cards, files or visitors books, but not odd scraps of paper), even if it is just names and contact details, then the Act applies to you. For the purposes of the Act you are a 'data controller'.

I think the Act applies to me. What must I do?

The three basic requirements are set out below. Please note that even if you are exempt from (a), you still need to comply with (b) and (c).

(a) Notify the Information Commissioner

- **No:** if you hold personal data on a manual filing system only, you do not need to notify.
- **Yes:** if you hold personal data on a computer (or any other automated system), you must notify unless you fall within one of the exemptions below.

Exemptions: you do **not** need to notify if you are only holding personal data for one or more of the following core business purposes:

- advertising, marketing and public relations, provided that:
  - you hold only the data necessary, on the people necessary for you to do your **own** advertising
  - you do not disclose the information to any third party not involved with your advertising without the consent of the person whose data it is
  - you only keep the personal information as long as is necessary to do the advertising
- staff administration (subject to similar conditions as advertising)
- accounts and financial records (subject to similar conditions as advertising).

How do I notify?

You notify the Commissioner using a standard form provided by the Information Commissioner's Office (see *Further guidance* below). The notification may also be done online. The details you need to provide include:

- your or your business's name and address
- a description of the purposes for which the data is being held, e.g. consultancy and advisory services
- a description of the data subjects on whom data is being held, e.g. customers and clients

- a description of the type of data being held, e.g. personal details
- a description of any person or organisation to whom you might disclose the data, e.g. employees.

There is an annual fee of £35.

The Information Commissioner's Office (ICO) has produced the helpful guidance booklet, *A Brief Guide to Notification*, which is free to download from their website **www.ico.org.uk**.

(b) Follow the data protection principles

All data controllers, whether their records are computerised, automated or manual, and whether they have to notify or not, must comply with the eight data protection principles set out in the Act. In brief, personal data should be:

- obtained and processed fairly and lawfully, and should not be held or used unless the data subject has given their consent, or it is necessary in performance of a contract to which the data subject is a party, or it is necessary for any other reason specified in the Act (see the *Direct Marketing* section)
- obtained only for specified and lawful purposes
- adequate, relevant and not excessive in relation to the purposes for which they are being held or used
- accurate and, where necessary, kept up to date
- kept no longer than necessary for the purposes concerned
- processed in accordance with the rights of data subjects (see (c) below)
- subject to appropriate technical and organisational measures against unauthorised or unlawful processing, and against accidental loss or destruction
- not transferred to a country or territory outside the European Economic Area, unless that country or territory ensures adequate levels of protection for the rights and freedoms of data subjects in relation to processing personal data.

Consent
Normally, if you are going to hold information on a guest for any purpose other than handling the booking, such as later marketing, you need to obtain consent.

The Act does not specify what form this consent has to be in, it may be an informal, spoken 'yes', but you should give guests enough information for them to make an informed decision (e.g. what personal information you intend to hold and why).

Guests can give their consent on booking, when they check in or when they check out. You should keep all consents on record.

You may want to produce a simple form that can be used either over the telephone, on e-mails or in writing, which:

- explains to guests the personal information on them you want to hold and why
- asks guests for their consent
- has a space to record whether or not consent was given.

If you intend to keep 'sensitive personal information', you must have the guest's explicit consent to hold and use their personal data for the purposes specified. Sensitive personal information includes the following:

- race, ethnic origins
- religion
- political opinions
- physical or mental health (e.g. disability)
- sexual orientation
- criminal convictions or allegations.

(c) Complying with the rights of data subjects

All data controllers must comply with the rights given to individuals by the Act in relation to the personal information held on them. The Act gives eight distinct rights, of which the most applicable are as follows:

- **Right of access**: individuals have a right to know what information on them you are holding and why you are holding it, although you are allowed to charge up to £10 to provide the person with this information. If you receive a written request from an individual for this information (with any relevant fee), you must respond within 40 days stating:
  - whether you hold any personal data on them
  - what the data is, the reason you are holding it and those to whom it has/may be disclosed, along with an intelligible copy of the information and details of the manner in which it was collected.
- **Right to prevent processing for the purposes of direct marketing**: if you receive a written request from an individual to cease using the personal data you hold on them for direct marketing, you must do so.
- **Right to prevent processing likely to cause damage or distress**: if you receive a written request from an individual to cease using the personal data you hold on them, because it is causing or likely to cause substantial damage or distress to them or another, you must do so.

- **Right to compensation**: any individual who suffers damage or distress as a result of a contravention of the Act by you is entitled to seek compensation from you if you did not take reasonable care to comply.

Note: you have the right to require reasonable proof of identity from a person asking to exercise these rights. You should be satisfied that the person asking is the person concerned, but you must not use excessive identity checking as a way to deliberately make access to the data difficult.

Caution! If you are buying in any mailing lists, you should ensure that the provider has the consent of the individuals listed to pass on the individual's details to third parties.

Data security and credit cards

The **Data Protection Act 1998** says that 'appropriate technical and organisational measures shall be taken against unauthorised or unlawful processing of personal data and against accidental loss or destruction of, or damage to, personal data.'

If you never receive a customer's card number (i.e. you use a third party to deal with transactions) you probably have little to worry about other than to ensure that the third party is a reputable organisation with a good knowledge of data security issues (e.g. Paypal or Worldpay).

If you do receive customers' data, you should follow the standards of the Payment Card Industry Security Standards Council **www.pcisecuritystandards.org**. This Council is a global consortium of all the main card payment companies including Mastercard and Visa. Its function is to promote standards of data security so as to make it harder for criminals to steal data. These standards are quite demanding, but compliance is mandatory for retailers who accept card payments. The requirements of the **Payment Card Industry Data Security Standard** are contractual rather than the law of the land but, if you follow them, you will also be meeting the legal requirement.

If you do handle card data you need to be sure that you know and follow those rules that are applicable to your circumstances. There are twelve requirements, some of which are of limited relevance to small businesses:

1 **Install and maintain a firewall**. Your computer operating system probably has this built in, e.g. Windows Firewall.

2 **Do not use default passwords**. If your password is "password", change it. Passwords should not be obvious.

3 **Protect stored cardholder data**. Do not leave personal data on your laptop and then travel with it, due to the risk of losing it. Keep it secure at all times.

4 **Encrypt internet transmission of cardholder data**. Never use ordinary e-mail to send credit card information.

5 **Use and regularly update anti-virus software**. This really is essential for everyone – set it to update automatically if you can.

6 **Develop and maintain secure systems and applications**. Likely to apply only to larger businesses developing their own systems.

7 **Restrict access to cardholder data on a need-to-know basis**. Ensure card data is not available to all your visitors, staff etc.

8 **Assign a unique ID to each person with computer access**. Do not share identities or passwords or run a database of past clients shared between several people with the same login.

9 **Restrict physical access to cardholder data**. Don't leave a print-out of data in an unlocked location (or a file of manual card data records).

10 **Track and monitor all access to network resources and cardholder data**. This is relevant to businesses with larger systems, but all businesses should record who has access to card data.

11 **Test security systems and processes regularly**. At the least, check that your security measures are being adhered to.

12 **Maintain a policy that addresses information security**. For small businesses the key point is that you give this topic some serious thought, rather than writing a formal policy.

For small accommodation providers, the above list can be summarised as making sure that access to card data, both on paper and electronically, is very well controlled, restricted to people who really need it, and that any computer on which you store it has proper defences such as a firewall and anti-virus software.

Further guidance

- The Information Commissioner's Office (ICO) helpline is: 0303 123 1113.
- There is also extensive information on the ICO's website **www.ico.gov.uk**

LICENCES & CONSENTS

MARKETING

GUESTS

FOOD & DRINK

HEALTH & SAFETY

STAFF

BUSINESS MANAGEMENT & TAX

FURTHER INFORMATION

Pricing and Charging

KEY FACTS

- It is a criminal offence for accommodation providers, among others, to give guests misleading information on the prices charged for accommodation and any related facilities, services or goods.
- It is an offence not to do everything reasonably possible to correct a price indication that has subsequently become misleading if it is reasonable to assume that customers will still be relying on the original price information.
- Prices must include VAT if you are VAT registered.

Price statements

Does this apply to me?

Almost certainly yes: as the Consumer Protection from Unfair Trading Regulations 2008 (CPRs)) covers all statements of price. It will normally apply to all accommodation providers whether the price is:
- stated in an advertisement, a brochure, a leaflet or on the web
- given in an email or text message
- given by letter or orally in person or over the telephone.

What does the Legislation require?

It is a criminal offence for you to give guests misleading information on the prices charged for accommodation and any related facilities, services or goods.

It is also an offence not to do everything reasonably possible to correct a price indication that has subsequently become misleading if it is reasonable to assume that customers will still be relying on the original price information.

Good practice

The Department for Business Innovation and Skills (BIS) has published a *Pricing Practices Guide – Guidance for traders on good practice in giving information about prices* which is available on the

Gov.uk website. This gives practical guidance on how to avoid giving misleading prices. Compliance with the Code, while not an absolute defence, will tend to assist you in showing that you have not committed an offence under the Act.

Taking the example of hotels and restaurants, the Code suggests that, as far as possible, all non-optional extras (such as a service charge) should be included in the price and accompanied by a clear statement about what the price includes.

The Code also says that all prices given to customers should include VAT. The message is that customers should not get any surprises when it comes to paying the bill.

Displaying prices on your premises

The **Consumer Protection from Unfair Trading Regulations 2008** (CPRs) require you to be open and honest in your pricing and not mislead or leave out information that could affect the purchasing decision of your customers (see *Unfair Trading Practices* for further information).

While there is no specific regulatory requirement regarding the display of prices in the reception, it is recommended that you do so in order to fulfill your obligations under the CPRs. This price list should be in a prominent position and be easy to read. It should include the price of:
- a bedroom for one person (single)
- a bedroom for two people (double)
- a bed in any other type of room.

All prices must include VAT and any compulsory service charge. You must make it clear if meals are included in the price.

Bonds/card payments in case of damage

The practice of taking bonds (or damage deposits) as protection against damages when accepting a booking is becoming more uncommon, as businesses are tending to retain customers' credit or debit card details in case of damage. If you wish to either charge a bond or to retain customers' card details so that you can charge for any damages, you must notify customers of this prior to the booking being agreed (while this can be done verbally, it is far better to do it in writing in case there is any dispute).

It is important to note that you are only able to retain money from the bond or charge a customers' card if the damage has resulted from a deliberate act (e.g. kicking in walls) or negligence (actions whereby it was reasonably foreseeable that damage would occur). You are not able to charge for damage that results from general 'wear and tear', e.g. marks on floors, an electrical item failing or cup breaking during washing-up.

To protect against disputes if a bond is retained, it is good practice to show a customer around a place so that any pre-existing damage can be recognised and agreed (as car hire companies do) and to get photographic evidence of any damage so this can be used to support a claim against a bond. Also, three quotes should be gained on any repairs to show that the amount of bond being retained is justified.

Finally, it is important to note that the requirement for guests to provide a bond or pay for damages must be applied in a fair and consistent manner that does not breach anti-discrimination law. That is, the requirement should be imposed on all guests and cannot just be imposed on the basis of race, disability, sexual orientation, age or gender. For example, you cannot require a bond from a group of young male customers if you do not require it from other groups of customers.

Further guidance

- URN 08/918: *Pricing Practices Guide: Guidance for traders on good practice in giving information about prices* can be downloaded from the **www.Gov.uk** website.
- Contact the Trading Standards office of your local authority for further advice.

Cancellations and No-shows

KEY FACTS

- All accommodation providers are strongly recommended to have a cancellation procedure, in order to avoid any problems with cancellation, curtailment and no-shows.
- If a guest cancels a booking or checks out early, they are in breach of the booking contract they have with you.
- If you have to cancel a booking that you have already accepted, you are in breach of the booking contract.

Cancellation by guests

Cancellation provisions in the booking conditions

To avoid any problems with cancellation or curtailment (when a guest cuts their stay short), you are strongly recommended to have a cancellation policy. To rely on the procedure you must make this policy clear to guests **before** you agree the booking, whether on the telephone, by fax, by e-mail or in writing. It is also prudent to get confirmation from the guests that they understand and accept the policy. Finally, your booking conditions and cancellation policy should also be clearly stated on your website.

It is recommended to include a cancellation clause in your standard booking terms and conditions (see the Bookings section). Common cancellation procedures are to either charge guests a cancellation fee that varies according to the amount of notice given of cancellation or to forfeit any deposit provided at the time of booking.

On cancellation or curtailment, you will need to send an invoice to the guest for the amount due. The amount due should be exclusive of VAT (as no services have been provided) and less any deposit that you have retained. It should also be noted that, if a customer has cancelled, no VAT on the cancellation fee is payable to HMRC. If VAT has already been paid on the deposit, this can be reclaimed from HMRC.

Cancellation insurance

One option that is often given to guests on booking is to take out cancellation insurance. A premium covers any payments they are obliged to make for their accommodation in the event of them having to cancel. A typical policy will cover claims as a consequence of illness or injury to the guest or a member of their family, redundancy, a burglary or fire or jury service.

If you need to comply with the **Package Travel Regulations** (see the *Holiday Packages* section), you are required to tell the guest about the possibility of taking out cancellation insurance in good time before the start of their holiday.

You can contact a local insurance company or broker for details of how to offer this facility.

Deposits

Increasingly, accommodation providers are taking deposits or asking for credit card details to reduce their exposure to cancellations.

People tend to expect self-catering owners to ask for a deposit. These establishments often charge a 25% deposit at the time of booking. They also typically request the balance between six to eight weeks in advance of arrival, to avoid being left with gaps they can't fill.

If you are VAT registered, you need to remember that any deposit is inclusive of VAT. This means that if you withhold a deposit as compensation for a guest cancelling, you must return the VAT component of the deposit as no service has been provided.

If a guest cancels and refuses to pay

If the guest refuses to pay:
- you may be able to charge the amount to their credit or debit card (as explained below), but if not:
- you will need to consider taking the matter to the small claims court.

Charging a credit card following cancellation or no-show

If you accept a telephone booking made by a credit or debit card and the guest later cancels the booking or fails to turn up, you can charge the guest's card **provided that** you can show that you have clearly communicated to the guest at the time the booking is made that their account will be charged in the case of a cancellation and the guest has accepted this condition.

One way to do this is to include this condition in your cancellation policy within the booking terms and conditions. Ideally, you should

LICENCES & CONSENTS   MARKETING   GUESTS   FOOD & DRINK   HEALTH & SAFETY   STAFF   BUSINESS MANAGEMENT & TAX   FURTHER INFORMATION

confirm this arrangement in writing or, at least, keep a record of the conversation as proof for the credit card company should the guest later challenge the charge. If the guest refuses to acknowledge having made a booking or claims they were not made aware of your cancellation conditions, and there is no proof to the contrary, banks will tend to refund their money, debiting your account. If you take bookings via the internet, it is a good idea to have a 'tick-box' where the guest has to confirm that they have read and accepted the cancellation conditions.

Claiming damages if a guest cancels

If a guest cancels a booking or checks out early, they are in breach of the booking contract they have with you. You may be entitled to claim damages for any losses you have suffered from the cancellation/curtailment. This applies regardless of whether or not you have cancellation/curtailment procedures as a booking condition.

Procedure

If you want to make a claim for damages, the procedure is as follows:

- **Re-letting the room**: You must first make every reasonable effort to minimise your loss by trying to re-let the accommodation. If you re-let the room at the same price, you should have not suffered a loss and so cannot make a claim.
- **What amount can I claim?** If, despite your efforts, you cannot re-let the accommodation, you will be entitled to claim damages that reflect the losses you have incurred as a result of the cancellation. This is the value of the booking or the part of it for which the accommodation could not be re-let, less the cost of any items that you did not supply. For example, you cannot charge for food, heating, electricity or cleaning as you did not supply these products or services. You are also not able to include any service charge.

Note: there is a general rule of thumb that your loss will be about two-thirds of the value of the booking, but individual cases differ.

- **What about the deposit?** You may keep the deposit, setting it off against the amount claimed.
- **How soon can I make a claim?** You must wait until the period of the booking has elapsed before you can send the guest an invoice for the amount claimed (this should be exclusive of VAT, as no services have been provided).
- **What happens if the guest does not pay the claim?** If you have any difficulties with a guest refusing to meet your claim, you could consider pursuing the claim through the small claims

procedure in the County Court. A small claim can be for any amount up to £10,000. You will have to pay a fee to start your claim which is related to the size of your claim, but this will be added to the money that you are already owed. The appropriate forms and a booklet advising you on how to pursue your claim can be obtained from any County Court.

What if a guest does not accept the accommodation?
Should a guest refuse to accept the accommodation booked or to accept any suitable alternative accommodation that you may offer, then, depending on the reasons given by the guest, you may be able to treat this as a cancellation.

Generally, you will not be able to do this if the guest rejects the accommodation because they booked it on the basis of untrue statements made about it by you or your staff or if the alternative accommodation does not meet the criteria of the guest's booking (eg. the guest specifically asked for a room with a sea view when booking and the only room available when they arrive overlooks the carpark).

What if I cancel a guest's booking?

If you have to cancel a booking that you have already accepted, you are in breach of contract. If you cannot accommodate a guest who has made a booking, you must find them alternative accommodation of the same or higher standard.

The guest is entitled to claim damages as compensation for any losses incurred in finding alternative comparable accommodation (e.g. extra taxi fares or any extra accommodation costs). However, the guest has a legal duty to keep losses to a minimum, so if your establishment is a bed and breakfast they cannot book into a five star hotel and expect you to pay the difference.

Further guidance

If you have any detailed questions on cancellations or any problems with a guest, you are advised to seek professional legal advice. Your local Trading Standards office may also be able to offer guidance.

www.visitengland.com/pinkbookonline

Accepting Guests

KEY FACTS

- Your rights with regard to accepting guests depend on whether you are classed as a 'hotel' or a 'private hotel'.
- A hotel can refuse guests who appear unable or unwilling to pay or who are not in a fit state to be received.
- A private hotel is free to pick and choose its guests even when rooms are available, provided that in exercising this right there is no discrimination as per the terms of the law.

Can I pick and choose my guests?

In certain instances, the law treats establishments offering serviced accommodation as either 'hotels' or 'private hotels'. The distinction between the two will affect your rights with regard to accepting guests, liabilities for guests' belongings and the ability to retain guests' luggage in the event that their bill is not paid (see the *Luggage and Belongings* section).

Note: whether you are a hotel or a private hotel, when the guest has made a prior booking, you must honour the booking unless there are legal grounds for not doing so, such as if you had accepted the booking on the basis of false statements made by the guest. For example, you state that pets are not allowed at your establishment and the guest arrives with a dog. In this sort of case, you can turn the guests away and you may also be able to claim damages from them if you are unable to re-let the room.

Are you a 'hotel' or a 'private hotel'?
A **hotel** is an establishment that offers food, drink and sleeping accommodation to anybody who appears able and willing to pay and who is in a fit state to be received. 'Drink' does not have to be alcoholic.

A **private hotel** is any accommodation establishment that is not a hotel. For example, you will be a private hotel if **any** of the following apply to you:
- guests can only book in advance
- you do not provide food and/or drink
- you pick and choose your guests, even if you have a free room
- you have an advertised policy that restricts certain guests (e.g. 'no children' or 'no coaches').

Can I turn guests away if I run a hotel?
If you are a hotel, you may only refuse to let a room to a prospective guest if that guest appears unable or unwilling to pay, or is not in a fit state to be received. This would be the case, for example, if the guest was drunk or if you had reasonable grounds for believing that the guest would be a nuisance to other guests.

However, you have complete discretion to decide which room to allocate to a guest, provided that the guest has not booked a specific room.

Can I turn guests away if I run a private hotel?
The proprietor of a private hotel is free to pick and choose their guests even when rooms are available, provided that in exercising this right they are not discriminating on the grounds set out by the law (see *Discrimination* below and the section on *Disabled Guests* for more information).

Discrimination
It is unlawful to discriminate against guests on the following 'protected characteristics':
- disability
- gender reassignment
- pregnancy and maternity
- race – this includes ethnic or national origins, colour and nationality
- religion or belief
- sex
- sexual orientation
- age – this applies to guests aged 18 and above, i.e. you cannot have a policy excluding under 25s.

Discrimination includes providing different standards of service, different products, charging different prices or having different terms and conditions.

However, you are allowed to provide different products and services for disabled guests provided that there is objective justification for

UPDATED

doing so. Objective justification is said to occur when the difference in goods or service provided is '**a proportionate means of achieving a legitimate aim**'. For example, it would probably be considered justified to only sell ground floor rooms in a listed building to someone in a wheelchair if the upper floors were only accessible by a staircase.

It should be noted that it is the inability to make alterations rather than the cost of making alternations that provides objective justification – i.e. you cannot provide a discriminatory service on the basis of cost alone.

In addition to not being able to discriminate against guests on the above grounds, you cannot discriminate against anyone on the grounds of association. This means not discriminating against the parent, partner, friend or carer accompanying someone with one of the protected characteristics listed above.

Indirect Discrimination
You must be careful not to have booking conditions or rules that would constitute indirect discrimination. Indirect discrimination occurs when any requirement, which in itself is not discriminatory, would have a disproportionate impact on people with a protected characteristic. For example, if you have a requirement that all male groups had to pay a higher booking fee because you had problems with stag parties in the past, this could be deemed to be indirect discrimination as it would always apply to gay couples but would not apply to heterosexual couples.

To help ensure that you do not discriminate, you are required to undertake reasonable adjustments to your premises or to the way you deliver your services. This, for example, could mean providing improved access, undertaking training for staff on equality issues or providing meals that comply with the religious requirements of guests.

Children
Anyone under the age of 18 does not have the same legal capacity as an adult to enter into a contract, such as making a room booking. You can accept bookings for someone under 18 to stay, but you are advised to be careful. For example, the booking itself should be made by someone 18 or over, whether a parent or guardian or another adult who can take responsibility for payment or damages.

If you would like more information about how this area of law affects you, there is a good service on the website of the Children's Legal Centre **www.childrenslegalcentre.com**, which answers questions in relation to children and the law.

UPDATED

LICENCES & CONSENTS   MARKETING   GUESTS   FOOD & DRINK   HEALTH & SAFETY   STAFF   BUSINESS MANAGEMENT & TAX   FURTHER INFORMATION

Disabled Guests

KEY FACTS

- If you provide any sort of accommodation, serviced or self-catering, the **Equality Act 2010** applies to you (this act replaces the **Disability Discrimination Act 1995**).

- The Act protects anyone who is disabled, is thought to be disabled or is associated with someone who is disabled.

- The Act gives these people rights of access to goods, facilities and services (including tourist accommodation) and ensures that they are treated no less favourably than other customers.

- You are also required to make reasonable adjustments to the way you deliver your services and to the physical features of your premises to make it easier for disabled guests to use them.

The Equality Act 2010

The **Equality Act 2010** was introduced to consolidate and strengthen all anti-discrimination legislation (including disability discrimination legislation). The Act builds on the **Disability Discrimination Act 1995** (DDA) which gives disabled people rights of access to goods, facilities and services, which includes tourist accommodation, by specifically banning discrimination against people associated with disabled people (e.g. carers, friends and family) and people presumed to be disabled. These rights are enforceable by any individual through the Courts, if necessary.

Does the Act apply to me?
Yes: if you provide any sort of accommodation, serviced or self-catering, the Act applies to you.

How is 'disabled' defined?
For the purpose of the law, people with disabilities are all those whose physical and mental impairments have a substantial and long-term adverse effect on their ability to carry out normal, day-to-day activities.

This includes those who have progressive conditions such as cancer, HIV and AIDS, multiple sclerosis, muscular dystrophy and who are likely to become increasingly disabled by their illness over time. These people become covered by the Act from the time they are diagnosed.

Note: a disability may not always be apparent so it is important not to make assumptions.

Types of discrimination

There are four types of disabled discrimination covered by the Equality Act. They are:
- direct discrimination
- indirect discrimination
- discrimination arising from a disability
- discrimination by association.

Direct discrimination

This is discrimination directly associated with a person's disability. As a 'service provider', you need to make sure you treat disabled guests the same as you treat other guests. You would be treating guests with disabilities less favourably if you:
- refuse to serve them
- offer less favourable terms
- offer a lower standard of service compared with what you normally offer.

It is important to note that the **Equality Act** does not allow any justification for direct discrimination. If you treat someone less favourably, the Act allows them to seek damages from you through the County Court.

Example of unequal treatment: discrimination would occur if a guest house refuses to give a room to someone who is mentally impaired on the basis that they feel the guest would upset other guests.

Indirect discrimination

This is where a business policy, while applying to all customers, would have a differential impact on disabled customers. Examples would include:
- serving breakfast only in a room that is down a set of stairs
- only accepting written orders for breakfast.

The Equality Act does allow indirect discrimination if there is 'objective justification'. For example, it may be justified to only allocate loft rooms to people who are not able to move unescorted on the grounds of fire safety. If there is no objective justification (cost is generally not acceptable), then reasonable adjustments (see below) need to be undertaken to adapt to the circumstances of the disabled customer. For example, allowing mobility-impaired customers to have their breakfast in their room or elsewhere in the hotel.

Discrimination arising from a disability
This is where the discrimination is based on a consequence of the disability rather than the disability itself. Examples would include:
- banning a person with Tourette's syndrome from a bar area because their outbursts may offend other customers
- providing plastic cups and plates to a person with muscular dystrophy because you think that they might break items.

Discrimination by association
This is discrimination against someone associated with a disabled person such as a carer, friend or member of the family. Examples may include:
- refusing the booking of a non-disabled couple because it was known they have a disabled child who they might bring with them
- making the carer of a disabled person sleep in the same room to ensure that they don't disturb other guests.

How does the Act impact on me?
To ensure that you do not discriminate against disabled people or their associates, the law requires you to make reasonable adjustments to both your property and your business practices.

Reasonable adjustments
Make **reasonable** adjustments to the way you deliver your services to make it easier for disabled guests to use them. This may include:
- changing the relevant underlying practice, policy, or procedure to make it easier
- providing an alternative method of making your services available
- getting training to use the Text Relay phonecall relay service or install a textphone (or 'Minicom') on the reception desk to allow customers with hearing impairments to make bookings more easily. Text Relay is an initiative providing text-to-voice translation to enable people who cannot hear or speak to connect with other people by phone. Visit **www.textrelay.org**.

Since 1 October 2004 'service providers' have had a duty to take reasonable steps to remove, alter or avoid any physical barriers that make it impossible or unreasonably difficult for disabled people to make full use of facilities, if the service cannot be provided by an alternative method.

What is reasonable?
You are only required to do what is 'reasonable'. The Equality and Human Rights Commission's (EHRC) Code of Practice gives more information on assessing whether a particular adjustment is reasonable. In general, the factors to consider would include:
- whether the proposed adjustment would meet the needs of the disabled person
- whether the adjustment is affordable
- whether the adjustment would have a serious effect on other people.

The Act permits service providers to justify less favourable treatment (and in some instances failure to make a reasonable adjustment) when there is no possibility to do so, despite the fact that this would mean that a disabled person is treated less favourably. Service providers do therefore have flexibility when considering how to make their services accessible to disabled people. Remember that what might be considered reasonable for a national hotel chain may not be so for a small guesthouse.

Examples of reasonable adjustments
- You could provide a bell at the main entrance to request assistance.
- You could provide large-print menus for visually-impaired guests.

Often simple measures can make your facilities more accessible, e.g. taking more time to help disabled guests, letting them know how to ask for help, and arranging appropriate training for you and your staff.

Before you make any changes, it is advisable to check with disability organisations that your adjustments are appropriate.

Note: even if you do not allow guests to bring their pets to your premises, you **must** allow people who need to use assistance dogs (such as visually impaired people) to be accompanied by their dogs.

Making adjustments to your website
The need for reasonable adjustments also applies to your website, which may be the first point of contact for a person with a disability.

You can download guidelines about accessibility from the Web Accessibility Initiative **www.w3.org/WAI** – these may seem daunting, but remember that they are guidelines rather than a definitive list of changes you must make. Small changes can make a big difference, such as the option to increase or reduce the size of text on the site.

There is a free accessibility toolbar to test your site and perform basic checks available from **www.snapfiles.com** – search within the site for 'accessibility toolbar'.

The Royal National Institute for the Blind (RNIB) offers advice on providing information in accessible formats, published in the *See it Right* pack. In addition, the British Standards Institute has produced a standard for web accessibility (BS 8878) and PAS 78, a document which provides guidance on designing websites for inclusive design, particularly for disabled people **www.shop.bsigroup.com**.

Auxiliary aids and services
In addition, you are required to provide what are described in the Act as 'auxiliary aids and services' where these would help a disabled person. Text Relay or Minicom (mentioned above), or British Sign Language interpretation would qualify as such services.

Again the rule of reasonable adjustments applies.

Good practice
In terms of what you should do in relation to disabled guests, good practice includes:
- thinking and planning ahead
- not making assumptions based on stereotypes
- asking a disabled person or organisation what is required if you are in doubt
- respecting the dignity of your disabled guest
- establishing a positive policy and practices
- training staff accordingly.

Note: sometimes a willingness to help and an attentive ear are enough to make a difference. Disabled people will tell you what you need to do to help them best. Also bear in mind that accessibility is often about making compromises, as a feature that will make things easier for one person might make them more difficult for another.

Tax allowances

On 1 April 2008 changes were introduced to the tax treatment of disability-related improvements made to properties. HM Revenue and Customs (HMRC) provide guidance on the tax allowances available to hotel operators in complying with the DDA **www.hmrc.gov.uk/specialist/disability-act-guidance.htm**.

There are changes to the rates for Plant and Machinery Allowances (PMA), which are useful to most accommodation businesses. However, the tax relief on disability-related expenditure on the structure of buildings only applies to what the HMRC define as 'qualifying hotels', i.e. those that:

- have a minimum of 10 letting rooms, where the rooms are serviced (i.e. not self-catering)
- serve meals
- are open for at least four months between April and October.

Further guidance on what constitutes a 'qualifying hotel' is available at **www.hmrc.gov.uk/manuals/camanual/CA32401.htm**.

National Accessible Scheme

There is a scheme for serviced, self-catering and caravan park accommodation which recognises and identifies those places to stay that meet the needs of disabled people and provides guidance to operators on how to improve accessibility.

For further information visit VisitEngland's industry website **www.visitengland.com/nas**.

Access Statement

Honest and accurate information is needed by disabled guests and others with access requirements. This can be achieved by writing and making available an **Access Statement**, which describes the services, facilities and structure of your business.

An Access Statement is a clear, accurate, and above all honest description of the current facilities and services you offer, to enable a potential visitor to make an informed decision as to whether your business meets their particular access needs. It highlights any key areas that might be a barrier to access for some visitors, for example steps or stairs.

From April 2007 participants in the VisitEngland quality scheme have been required to prepare an Access Statement as part of their quality grading assessment. Participants need to present an Access Statement to the quality assessor at the time of their quality assessment visit.

Another related requirement is that Access Statements/accessibility information are made available to guests, helping the industry provide essential information to customers while fulfilling part of their legal obligation under the **Equality Act 2010**. VisitEngland recommends that the Access Statement is uploaded to the property website.

Go to **www.visitengland.com/access** for help and advice, an online tool to assist operators and best practice examples.

Further guidance

- VisitEngland provides guidance, tools and resources to help businesses with the access needs of customers
  www.visitengland.com/access
- For more information on the **Equality Act** and help with good business practice contact the Equality and Human Rights Commission Helpline (EHRC) on 0845 604 6610 (text phone 0845 604 6620). The EHRC's website is **www.equalityhumanrights.com**
- Tourism for All UK **www.tourismforall.org.uk** is a national registered charity which provides expertise and support to the tourism and hospitality sector to provide accessible services for all. Tel: 0845 124 9971 (information line).
- RNIB *See it Right* guidelines (Practical advice on designing, producing and planning for accessible information – product code PR12098), is available on CD at £15 by calling their helpline 0303 123 9999.
- Information and guidelines on best practice for customers with hearing loss is available from Action on Hearing Loss (formerly RNID) from **www.actiononhearingloss.org.uk**, information hotline 0808 8080 123.

Luggage and Belongings

KEY FACTS

- If you run serviced accommodation, you are required by law to take responsibility for the safekeeping of all reasonable items of luggage brought in by guests.
- Hotel owners have the legal right to retain guests' property until their bill is settled.

Rights and responsibilities

Depending on whether your property is classified as a 'hotel' or as a 'private hotel' (see *Accepting Guests* section) will have a bearing on:

- your responsibility for guests' luggage and belongings
- your right to keep guests' luggage.

Note: for these purposes, all serviced accommodation establishments are either hotels or private hotels.

What is a hotel and a private hotel?

- A **hotel** is an establishment that offers food, drink and sleeping accommodation to anybody who appears able and willing to pay, and who is in a fit state to be received.

  Note: 'drink' does not have to be alcoholic.

- A **private hotel** is any accommodation establishment that is not a hotel. For example, you will be a private hotel if **any** of the following apply to you:
  - you do not provide food and/or drink
  - you pick and choose your guests, even if you have a free room
  - you have an advertised policy of, for example, 'no children' or 'no coaches'
  - you can only book in advance.

What is the responsibility of a hotel for luggage and belongings?

If you run a hotel and you accept a guest into your accommodation for at least one night, you are required by law to take responsibility for the safekeeping of all reasonable items of luggage brought in by the guest. If the guest's property is then lost or damaged, the extent of your liability will vary as follows:

- **You may not be liable**, where the loss or damage to the guest's property is caused by an act of negligence on the part of the guest or by an 'Act of God' (such as a flood).
- **You may be fully liable**, where:
  - the loss or damage to the guest's property is caused solely by your negligence or wilful act (or that of your staff), or
  - the goods have been entrusted to you for your safekeeping, or
  - the goods have been offered to you for safekeeping but refused by you.
- **You may limit your liability to £50/£100**, where the loss or damage to the guest's property does not fit into either of the above categories and you have displayed the statutory notice set out below in a prominent area of your establishment (near the main entrance or reception area).

Note: under the **London Local Authorities Act 2004**, the limits in Greater London are £750 and £1,500 respectively.

The statutory notice is as follows (the second version of the notice is for Greater London only).

NOTICE: Loss of or damage to guests' property

Under the Hotel Proprietors' Act 1956, a hotel proprietor may in certain circumstances be liable to make good any loss of or damage to a guest's property even though it was not due to any fault of the proprietor or staff of the hotel. This liability however:

- extends only to the property of guests who have engaged sleeping accommodation at the hotel
- is limited to £50 for any one article and a total of £100 in the case of any one guest, except in the case of property which has been deposited, or offered for deposit, for safe custody
- does not cover motor cars or other vehicles of any kind or property lost in them, or horses or other live animals.

This notice does not constitute an admission either that the Act applies to this hotel or that liability thereunder attaches to the proprietor of this hotel in any particular case.

LONDON ONLY

NOTICE: Loss of or damage to guests' property

Under the Hotel Proprietors' Act 1956 and the London Local Authorities Act 2004, a hotel proprietor may in certain circumstances be liable to make good any loss of or damage to a guest's property even though it was not due to any fault of the proprietor or staff of the hotel. This liability however:

- extends only to the property of guests who have engaged sleeping accommodation at the hotel
- is limited to £750 for any one article and a total of £1,500 in the case of any one guest, except in the case of property which has been deposited, or offered for deposit, for safe custody
- does not cover motor cars or other vehicles of any kind or property lost in them, or horses or other live animals.

This notice does not constitute an admission either that the Act applies to this hotel or that liability thereunder attaches to the proprietor of this hotel in any particular case.

What if the guest did not stay overnight?

If you are a hotel and the guest did not stay overnight and was, for example, just visiting the restaurant or bar, the position is the same as in the paragraph below for private hotels.

What is your liability as a private hotel?

If your establishment is a private hotel, then you will usually be liable for the loss or damage to your guests' property only if you or your staff have been negligent or if the guest handed the property over to you for safekeeping.

It is difficult to be more specific regarding your liability to the loss to guests' property as each case depends on the circumstances of the loss or damage.

Your right to retain a guest's luggage

Owners of hotels

The owner of a hotel (see Definitions above) has the legal right to retain guests' property until they settle their bill. This right does not extend to the guest's car or property left in it, or to the clothes that the guest is wearing.

When the bill is paid, the property must be returned to the guest. No storage charge may be made and you must reimburse the guest accordingly if the property has been damaged while in your possession.

Selling guests' property
If the bill has not been paid in full after six weeks, you may then sell the guest's property. The sale must be by public auction and it must be advertised at least four weeks in advance in both a London and a local newspaper. The adverts must set out your intention to sell the property, give a full description of the goods, name the guest to whom they belonged and give full details of the forthcoming sale.

The proceeds of sale, less the amount owed to you and the costs of the advertisements and organising the auction, must then be returned to the guest on demand.

This right is in addition to any other right that you have, such as that of pursuing a claim for non-payment through the small claims court.

Note: you cannot detain a guest except to await the arrival of the police.

Owners of private hotels and self-catering accommodation
Private hoteliers who retain the right to pick and choose their guests have no legal right to retain and sell a guest's property, nor does a proprietor of self-catering accommodation.

If a guest does not pay a bill and further contact or correspondence does not result in payment, then you have the option of pursuing a claim for non-payment through the small claims court (see the *Cancellations and No-Shows* section).

Further guidance
For more detailed advice, or if a serious claim is made against you, you are advised to obtain professional legal advice.

Childcare

KEY FACTS

- If you regularly provide day care for children under the age of eight for more than two hours in any day, then registration with Ofsted may be necessary.

- The registration process involves filling in an application form and providing details about other people associated with the care.

- Ofsted will need to be satisfied that you are a suitable person, and will expect certain qualifications or recommend some training.

Childcare Facilities and the Children Act 1989

Under Part XA of the **Children Act 1989**, you are required to register with Ofsted if you are offering certain types of care facilities for children under the age of eight for more than two hours. This applies regardless of whether the child belongs to a member of staff (e.g. a crèche for employees) or a guest (e.g. a child-care service or kids' activity group).

Does this apply to me?

No: if the child is over the age of eight, or;
if the child is in your care for less than two hours

Yes: if the child is between five and eight years old and in your care for more than two hours – you have to be on the **Ofsted Child Care Register**
if the Child is under five years old and in your care for more than two hours – you have to be on the **Ofsted Early Years Register**.

You can apply to join one register or both registers at the same time. You can also apply for voluntary registration with Ofsted if you are offering childcare that does not need to be registered.

It is important to note that the Act says that you have a duty to ensure that the children are well cared for even if you are not required to be on a register.

Are baby-sitting and baby-listening services covered?

Baby sitting is not specifically covered by the Act. This is because care that is provided on the parent's own premises is not normally treated as childminding unless you care for the children of more than two sets of parents in the home of one of them.

Baby-listening services do not come within the scope of the Act. However, if you provide baby-sitting services on a regular basis on particular premises, such as a hotel's baby-sitting service, then you may need to register.

If you need to apply for registration, or are in any doubt as to whether you need to register, you should contact Ofsted.

Registration with Ofsted

In the first instance, you should contact your local authority for information about pre-registration briefings and an application pack. Ofsted recommends a briefing session with your local authority before making your application.

The registration process starts as soon as your form is received by Ofsted. They aim to complete the process within 12 weeks for childminders, and 25 weeks for day care providers.

During this time, Ofsted will arrange a registration visit and a 'suitable person' interview with one of their inspectors. They will carry out a number of checks, including with the Criminal Records Bureau, on everyone associated with an application such as the applicant, day care manager or those who live on the premises where the applicant proposes to provide child-minding.

The registration process is explained in the Ofsted leaflets mentioned below in *Further guidance*.

After registration, Ofsted will conduct a first inspection within seven months of you starting to care for children. Regular inspections of the quality of care follow this first inspection at least once every three years, and in some cases more often.

Training

The Department for Education's Early Years Foundation Stage (EYFS) is the statutory framework that sets the standards that all Early Years providers must meet to ensure that children learn and develop well and are kept healthy and safe. This is a comprehensive framework which sets the standards for learning, development and care of children from birth to five and was revised in 2014. All registered early years providers are required to use the EYFS.

Further guidance

- For advice on all aspects of registration, contact the Ofsted helpline on: 0300 123 1231
- The Ofsted website gives information on registration for day care providers and childminders **www.ofsted.gov.uk**
- The *Early Years Foundation Stage* can be downloaded from Foundation Years website **www.foundationyears.org.uk/eyfs-2014/**.

FOOD & DRINK

Food Safety and Hygiene

KEY FACTS

- If you supply food to guests you must comply with the provisions of food safety and hygiene legislation. The word 'food' is defined as including drink.
- You should not provide food that is unsafe (i.e. injurious to health) or unfit for human consumption.
- You must implement a food safety management system to ensure that the food you provide is safe to eat. These procedures must be based on the HACCP principles.
- You must not keep foods at a temperature that might make them unsafe to eat. There are specified temperatures that different hot or chilled foods must be kept at.
- Registration with the local authority is required for accommodation businesses that serve or supply food or drink of any description, including bed and breakfasts.

Food safety legislation

The most important food safety and hygiene legislation applying in the UK comprises of:

- legislation relating to the **hygiene of foodstuffs**, namely **EC Regulation No. 852/2004**, setting out the day-to-day requirements for food business operators
- legal requirements for **temperature controls**, as outlined in the **Food Hygiene (England) Regulations 2006** (as amended) (and equivalent regulations in other UK countries)
- the **enforcement provisions** for local authorities, as contained in the **Food Hygiene (England) Regulations 2006** (as amended) and the **Food Safety Act 1990** (as amended).

Does food safety legislation apply to me?

Yes: if you supply food to guests, you must comply with the provisions of the legislation. The word 'food' is defined as including drink.

Main provisions of the legislation
General Food Law Regulation (EC) 178/2002
Regulation (EC) 178/2002 covers the placing of unsafe or unfit food on the market. You should not place food on the market (that is to sell or supply food, or hold it with intent to supply) which is:
- unsafe (i.e. injurious to health)
- unfit for human consumption, e.g. food that is rotten, 'gone off' or has been subject to considerable contamination.

The Regulation also covers traceability. You should keep records of businesses which have supplied food to you and any businesses you supply food to. The Food Standards Agency (FSA) guidance says this should include:
- address of customer or supplier
- nature and quantity of products
- date of transaction and delivery.

This is to help when a food manufacturer needs to co-ordinate a withdrawal of unsafe food. There are offences for breaches of these provisions in the **General Food Regulations 2004** (as amended).

Offences under the Food Safety Act 1990
- **Rendering food injurious to health**. Not only is it an offence to place food on the market which is harmful to health, it is also an offence to do anything which would make food harmful by adding something to it or removing something from it. This may apply even if you did not realise the effect of what you were doing at the time.
- **Selling 'to the purchaser's prejudice' food which is not of the nature, substance or quality demanded**. 'To the purchaser's prejudice' means to his or her disadvantage. This includes things like supplying lemonade when low-calorie lemonade has been requested, or supplying a beef casserole when the customer has ordered lamb casserole.
- **Falsely or misleadingly describing, advertising or presenting food**. This offence can be committed when statements or pictures concerning food are untrue. It can also cover statements that are strictly speaking correct but presented in such a way that the customer is led to the wrong conclusion. Bearing this in mind, you should take care with the descriptions of dishes on your menus. There is a similar provision about this in the General Food Law Regulation.

General food hygiene

Do the Regulations apply to me?

Yes: if you are an accommodation provider that supplies food to guests, you must register with your local authority at least 28 days prior to trading and comply with the Regulations. It does not matter if you are a small bed and breakfast, a five-star hotel or you provide meals in other circumstances. As a food business operator, the onus is on you to make sure you supply safe food.

If you are not sure whether you should register as a food business, you should speak to your local environmental health department for advice.

How do I comply?

Food safety management procedures

You must put in place and implement a food safety management system to ensure that the food you provide is safe to eat. These procedures must be based on the HACCP principles, although they can be proportionate to the nature and size of the business and should not be burdensome on small businesses. HACCP stands for:

- **h**azard
- **a**nalysis
- **c**ritical
- **c**ontrol
- **p**oint.

This means that you must:

- analyse all potential **food hazards** – a hazard is anything that might hurt the consumer
- identify the **points in the operation** where hazards might occur
- decide which of the points identified are **critical** to ensuring food safety
- identify and implement effective **control and monitoring** procedures at those critical points
- determine what **corrective actions** must be taken if your procedures are not working
- keep appropriate **records** to show your procedures are working
- **review** all of the above periodically and whenever your food operations change.

Records

The amount of paperwork you will need to keep as part of your safety procedures will also depend on the size and nature of your business. Larger businesses will need to maintain some documented procedures in addition to their records.

LICENCES & CONSENTS

MARKETING

GUESTS

FOOD & DRINK

HEALTH & SAFETY

STAFF

BUSINESS MANAGEMENT & TAX

FURTHER INFORMATION

The Food Standards Agency offers a number of models to help you comply with the record-keeping part of the procedures (see 'Safer Food, Better Business' in *Further guidance* below.) You can also contact your local authority for advice.

Food premises

As a basic requirement, food premises must comply with the following:
- they must be kept clean, be well maintained and designed to enable good hygiene practices to be adhered to.
- they must have adequate hand-washing facilities available, with supplies of hot and cold water, and drying facilities suitably located and designated for cleaning hands. (Toilets must not open directly into rooms where food is handled).
- they must have adequate means of ventilation, lighting and drainage.

What is adequate in any situation will depend on the nature and size of the business.

In addition, the following requirements apply to all rooms in which food is prepared, except dining areas:
- surface finishes to walls, doors, floors and equipment should be easy to clean and, if necessary, to disinfect.
- there must be adequate facilities for cleaning work tools and equipment and for washing food.

Slightly scaled down, but broadly similar, requirements apply to premises that are only used occasionally for catering purposes.

The full list of requirements are detailed in the *Safer food, better business for caterers* section of the FSA website **www.food.gov.uk/business-industry/caterers/sfbb/sfbbcaterers**

Domestic premises

Premises 'used primarily as a dwelling house but where foods are regularly prepared' (i.e. this might include some bed and breakfasts) are subject to slightly different requirements with regard to the rooms where food is prepared (**Regulation (EC) 852/2004 Annex II Chapter III**). Speak to the Environmental Health Department of your local authority for guidance.

Further requirements

- **Equipment:** all equipment and other items which come into contact with food must be kept clean and well maintained and installed in such a way as to allow adequate cleaning of the surrounding area.
- **Food waste:** waste must not be allowed to accumulate and, as

a general rule, must be kept in closed containers which are easy to clean and disinfect. The waste must be eliminated in a hygienic and environmentally-friendly way and must not constitute a direct or indirect source of contamination.

- **Water supply:** there must be an adequate supply of drinking water. Generally, this water supply should be used to make sure that food is not contaminated and any ice should be made from it.
- **Cleaning agents:** cleaning chemicals must not be stored in areas where food is handled.
- **Personal hygiene:** everyone working with food must maintain a high level of personal cleanliness, including clean clothing. You must not allow anyone suffering from an illness which could contaminate food to work in a food handling area. Additionally, staff working in food handling areas are required to report such illnesses to you. You should also ensure that good hand washing routines are maintained.
- **Raw materials:** you should not buy, or supply, any raw material that will not be fit for human consumption.
- **Protection against contamination:** all food must be protected against any form of contamination, including pests, which would make it fail food safety requirements.
- **Training:** all staff handling food must receive training commensurate or appropriate to the work they do. The *Industry Guide to Good Hygiene Practice: Catering Guide* (currently being updated) states that:
  - high-risk food handlers such as those who prepare high-risk foods should hold a basic or foundation certificate (level 2)
  - a waiter/waitress would require hygiene awareness training (level 1)
  - the person responsible for implementing the food hygiene management system must have received adequate training to enable them to do this.

The full list of requirements are detailed in the FSA guide *Food Hygiene – A Guide for Businesses*.

Food and temperature control

The temperature control rules are found in the **Food Hygiene (England) Regulations 2006** (and equivalent legislation in Scotland, Wales and Northern Ireland).

Do the Regulations apply to me?

Yes: if you are an accommodation provider that offers food to guests, you must comply with the regulations. Just as with the hygiene regulations, it does not matter what type of premises you have – all food providers need to comply with the temperature requirements.

What are the requirements?

You must not keep foods at a temperature that might make them unsafe to eat.

Foods which need temperature control for safety must be held either:
- **hot** (at or above a minimum temperature of 63°C) or
- **chilled** (at or below a maximum temperature of 8°C).

In addition to this, foods that are likely to support the growth of harmful bacteria or the formation of toxins should not be kept at temperatures which would result in a risk to health.

Exemptions

Some foods are exempt from the 8°C limit, such as:
- bakery products which are to be used quickly
- most unopened canned foods
- dried foods
- food which is ripening or maturing at room temperature (e.g. soft cheeses).

Serving and display of food

The regulations also have a degree of flexibility in the serving and display of food. For example, food that should normally be kept at or below 8°C may be kept above that temperature for a single period of four hours to allow it to be served or displayed (e.g. food on a buffet table or cheese trolley). After this period it should either be thrown away or chilled back to 8°C or below until used.

Likewise, food which will be served hot may be kept on display out of temperature control (63°C and above) for a single period of two hours. If any food is left after this time, food should either be discarded, reheated to 63°C or above (in Scotland, food must be reheated to 82°C or above), or cooled as quickly as possible to 8°C or below until final consumption.

Guidance on temperature control legislation in the UK is available on the FSA website **www.food.gov.uk**.

Handling ready-to-eat foods safely

It is important to handle ready-to-eat foods carefully as they could, if mishandled, lead to cases of food poisoning. They include sandwiches, salads, desserts, cold cooked meats, and foods you have cooked in advance to serve cold. The following controls should prevent this from happening:

- check that the temperature of purchased frozen and chilled ready-to-eat foods is correct (under 8°C for chilled foods, -18°C for frozen foods)
- check products are within the date code and that the packaging is not damaged
- do not use products after their 'use by' date
- store ready-to-eat foods separately from raw foods, such as meat, poultry and eggs. Store at the correct temperature and rotate stock
- follow the manufacturer's instructions on storage and preparation
- wash and dry hands before the preparation of ready-to-eat foods
- use clean knives, utensils, and separate boards for the preparation of ready-to-eat foods
- sanitise boards, surfaces and utensils after use
- keep ready-to-eat foods covered after preparation
- once prepared do not allow ready-to-eat foods to remain at room temperature for any longer than necessary
- buy a thermometer to monitor temperatures.

Enforcement and food hygiene inspections

Local authorities are responsible for enforcing food hygiene laws and authorised enforcement officers have the right to enter and inspect food premises (registered or not) at any reasonable time without having to make an appointment – they will usually come without notice.

They carry out routine inspections and the frequency varies depending on the degree of risk posed by the business and its previous record. Inspectors may also visit as a result of a complaint.

Inspectors (i.e. 'authorised officers') will look at the way you operate your business to identify any potential hazards and to make sure that you are complying with the law. They will discuss problems with you and advise on possible solutions. They also have the following powers:

- to take samples and photographs and to inspect your records
- to write to you informally, asking you to rectify any problems that they have found. If a breach of the law has been identified, they may serve you with a 'hygiene improvement notice'
- to detain or seize suspect foods
- to recommend a prosecution (although this is normally done only in serious cases)

- to serve 'a hygiene emergency prohibition notice' which forbids the use of the premises or equipment (if there is an imminent health risk to the public). Such a notice must be confirmed by the Courts (or a Sheriff in Scotland).

Further guidance on food hygiene inspections is contained in the publication *Food law inspections and your business* which is available on the FSA website **www.food.gov.uk**.

Allergies

A small percentage of the population is allergic to, or intolerant of, certain foods. In the UK, it is estimated that around 2% of the population suffer from food allergies and each year some people become seriously ill and even die from extreme reactions to foods such as peanuts, shellfish and eggs.

Under the **Food Safety Act 1990** and the **General Food Law Regulation 178/2002** you are responsible for ensuring that the food that customers eat is safe and the quality is what they expect. This means you should understand exactly what foods can cause problems.

The following is a list of the 14 most common allergens. You must be aware of any use of these allergens in the food that you prepare and communicate this use to your customers (see section on *Food Labelling* for more information on your requirement to inform customers of any use of allergens in food you serve customers).

- cereals containing gluten
- crustaceans, for example prawns, crabs, lobster and crayfish
- eggs
- fish
- peanuts
- soybeans
- milk
- nuts, such as almonds, hazelnuts, walnuts, pecan nuts, Brazil nuts, pistachio, cashew and macadamia nuts
- celery (and celeriac)
- mustard
- sesame
- sulphur dioxide, which is a preservative found in some dried fruit
- lupin
- molluscs, for example clams, mussels, whelks, oysters, snails and squid.

UPDATED

'Scores on the Doors'

There has been a growing trend in recent years for local authorities to introduce schemes whereby their assessment of the business's compliance with food hygiene regulations is scored and published for consumer information. These schemes, commonly known as 'Scores on the Doors' schemes, have been introduced on the basis that if customers can see the extent to which an establishment complies with food hygiene legislation, then they can make an informed decision as to whether to eat in that establishment. This, in turn, is believed to provide a stimulus for businesses to improve their food hygiene practices.

The large number of different schemes and associated symbols used by different councils across Britain has resulted in concern that the public are confused when trying to compare the hygiene standards of premises in different locations. This resulted in the Food Standards Agency developing and introducing a National Food Hygiene Rating Scheme in November 2010. This scheme ranks the cleanliness of premises that sell food between '0' (meaning urgent improvement is needed) and '5' (meaning very good).

The National Food Hygiene Rating Scheme covers all businesses that supply food directly to consumers, so this will include hotels, bed and breakfasts, supermarkets, restaurants, cafés and takeaways.

Although not mandatory, the Food Standard Agency is steadily replacing most of the existing Scores on Doors schemes in England, Wales and Northern Ireland (a separate two-tier scheme operates in Scotland which has ratings of "pass" and "improvement needed") as councils gradually switch to it from their current schemes.

The National Scheme does not require councils to switch from their current scheme and many councils still use the alternative commercially run Scores on the Doors scheme which uses stars rather than numbers.

However, both schemes have two fundamental features:
- it is not mandatory for you to display the score that you have received (although this information will be available to the public on the local authority website)
- you have the ability to appeal against the score that you receive if you believe the manner in which it was derived to be unfair.

Further guidance

For information and advice about food safety and hygiene, or any Scores on the Doors scheme operating in your area, contact your local environmental health department.

The Food Standards Agency (FSA) was established in 2000. As a Government department, independent regulator and consumer protection body, it uses the best available evidence and works with:
- business from farm to fork to help them keep consumers safe
- local authorities and other food law enforcement bodies to help them take proportionate, timely and resolute action
- consumers, to provide reliable and up-to-date information to help them make healthy choices about food.

The FSA produces a range of useful publications which can be accessed from the Agency's home page by going to **www.food.gov.uk**. Some of the key publications include the following:
- *Starting Up: Your first steps to running a catering business.* Basic information for all businesses supplying food on a wide range of issues.
- *Food Hygiene – A Guide for Businesses.*
- *Safer Food, Better Business.* SFBB is an innovative and practical approach to food safety management. It has been developed to help small businesses put in place food safety management procedures and comply with food hygiene regulations.
- *Cooksafe*: FSA Scotland has drawn on expertise from the food industry including small businesses, local authorities and the Scottish Food Advisory Committee to develop a HACCP-based system called 'CookSafe'.
- *Advice for Caterers on Allergy and Intolerance.*
- *Food Law Inspections and Your Business.*
- For more information on the National Food Hygiene Rating Scheme visit **www.ratings.food.gov.uk**.

Food Labelling

KEY FACTS

- If you provide food for guests that contains GM ingredients you will need to comply with genetically modified food legislation.
- From 13 December 2014, you will need to provide information to customers on 14 allergens that may be used as ingredients in any food you sell.

Pricing food

For details on pricing food, see *Pricing and Charging*, page 50.

Food labelling and genetically modified food

To allow food providers and consumers alike to make informed decisions about the food they use or eat, there are food labelling regulations in place.

The rules covering GM foods are outlined in:
- the **European Regulations (EC) No. 1829/2004, (EC) No. 1830/2004**
- the **GM Food (England) Regulations 2004**
- the **Genetically Modified Organisms (Traceability and Labelling) Regulations 2004**
- (and equivalent Regulations in Scotland, Wales and Northern Ireland).

Do the Regulations apply to me?
- **No:** if there are no ingredients containing, consisting of, or produced from genetically modified organisms in the food you offer to guests, the regulations do not apply to you.
- **Yes:** if you are providing food for guests that contains ingredients containing, consisting of, or produced from genetically modified organisms, whether or not there is any GM material in the final product (e.g. oil produced from GM soya

or maize), you need to comply. Any intentional use of GM must be labelled, but there is a tolerance level (of 0.9%) for the accidental inclusion of EU-authorised GM material. For further information, see **www.food.gov.uk/science/novel/gm/ gm_labelling#.U33km_ldV1c**.

As any food bought by you to prepare food for guests should be similarly labelled for GM ingredients, you should be able to tell whether or not you need to comply.

What do the Regulations require?
The words 'genetically modified' or 'produced from genetically modified [name of organism]' must be displayed on a notice, menu, ticket or label which can be easily read by customers. For example:
*Products on the menu marked * contain ingredients produced from genetically modified soya.*

Allergies and labelling
It is estimated that around 2% of the population suffer from food allergies and each year some people become seriously ill and even die from extreme reactions to foods such as peanuts, shellfish and eggs.

Under the **Food Safety Act 1990** and the **General Food Law Regulation 178/2002** you are responsible for ensuring that the food that customers eat is safe and the quality is what they expect. This means you should understand exactly what foods can cause problems.

The 14 most common allergens in Europe are:
- cereals containing gluten
- crustaceans, for example prawns, crabs, lobster and crayfish
- eggs
- fish
- peanuts
- soybeans
- milk
- nuts, such as almonds, hazelnuts, walnuts, pecan nuts, Brazil nuts, pistachio, cashew and macadamia nuts
- celery (and celeriac)
- mustard
- sesame
- sulphur dioxide, which is a preservative found in some dried fruit
- lupin
- molluscs, for example clams, mussels, whelks, oysters, snails and squid.

Packaged Food

You are legally required to supply information on the labels of pre-packaged food when any of the 14 allergens listed above are included as an ingredient. Any use of these allergens must be highlighted in the ingredients list. This means that having notices on signs or other parts of the packaging that say, for example, 'contains nuts' is not permitted.

Unpackaged Food

Currently, you don't have to provide information on allergens for food served without packaging or upon a customer's request (e.g. food served in restaurants).

However, this will change from **13 December 2014**. From this date, you will need to provide information to customers on any of the 14 allergens used as ingredients in foods sold without packaging or wrapped on site. This information could be written down on a chalk board or menu, or provided orally by a member of staff. Where the specific allergen information is not provided upfront, clear signposting to where this information could be obtained must be provided (i.e. a note on your menu telling customers to ask a waiter regarding the use of allergens in any of the items on the menu).

It is therefore very important that your staff are trained and regularly updated on the use of any allergens in food that you serve.

These rules will only cover information about major allergens intentionally used as ingredients. They do not cover allergens present following accidental contact.

Further guidance

- Further information on GM foods, food allergies and intolerance is available from the Food Standard Agency website **www.food.gov.uk**
- Contact your local trading standards department for more information on food labelling.

Health and Safety at Work Act

KEY FACTS

- The Health and Safety at Work Act (HSWA) places general duties and responsibilities on all people at work, including employers, employees and the self-employed.
- You are responsible for ensuring, so far as is reasonably practicable, the health, safety and welfare of all your employees at work plus anyone else who could be affected by your work activities, e.g. guests, casual workers, contractors.
- Your employees also have a responsibility to take reasonable care of their own health and safety.
- If you employ more than five people you must have a written health and safety policy.
- You must carry out a risk assessment to identify and manage any risks.

Your responsibilities as an employer to employees and others

The **Health and Safety at Work Act 1974** (HSWA) sets the framework for health and safety regulations in the workplace. The Act places general duties and responsibilities on all people at work, including employers, employees and the self-employed. There are two important responsibilities for an employer:

- you are responsible for ensuring, so far as is reasonably practicable, the health, safety and welfare of all your employees at work (your employees also have a responsibility to take reasonable care of their own health and safety)
- you have a wider responsibility to ensure, again so far as is reasonably practicable, the safety of other people who are affected by your business, for example guests, their children and visitors, a casual worker or a contractor.

All the health and safety legislation covered in this service relates to employers, employees, the self-employed and the workplace. The provisions do not normally apply to self-catering accommodation owners unless they have employees working on their premises, e.g. doing cleaning or maintenance work. If you have an employee, the legislation is applicable whether or not that employee is at work, and whether or not the employee works at the premises concerned. In other words, if you employ anyone at all, you are an employer, and you must comply with the Act in the management of your whole business.

Health and safety law seldom prescribes specific rules for you to follow. Far more often it requires you to manage safety for yourself, and there are severe penalties for not doing so, which, since January 2009, include the possibility of a jail sentence. It is mandatory that you devote time and careful attention to the management of safety in your business; this is at the heart of the law and you cannot fulfil your legal duties by form-filling or cursory treatment of the topic.

Additional health and safety legislation

Other health and safety legislation supplements the HSWA's general responsibilities with specific requirements. The key regulations are covered in this service publication – see the following sections:

- *Fire Safety (General)* see page 125
- *Fire Safety of Furniture and Furnishings* see page 133
- *Safety Management* see page 96
- *Hazards in the Workplace* see page 108
- *Hazards from Work Activities* see page 102
- *Swimming, Gym and Outdoor Safety* see page 121.

Policy statement and risk assessment

- If you employ five or more people, you must have a written health and safety policy that includes the arrangements for management of safety in your business.
- Your health and safety arrangements will come from doing a risk assessment to identify any risks and then making decisions on how to manage such risks, so far as is reasonably practicable, to comply with health and safety law.
- If you employ five or more employees, you must record:
  - the significant findings of the assessment
  - any group of employees identified by it as being especially at risk.

Even if you do not employ five people, it is still good practice to make a written record of your assessment. If you do not, it may later be difficult to demonstrate that a suitable and sufficient risk assessment has been carried out.

For information about how to do a risk assessment see the *Safety Management* section (page 96).

Health and safety notices

You are required to display the *Health and Safety Law poster* if you employ anyone **www.hse.gov.uk/contact/faqs/lawposter.htm**.

Alternatively you can provide your employees with individual copies of the same information in a leaflet entitled *Your Health and Safety - A Guide for Workers* **www.hse.gov.uk/pubns/indg450.htm**.

Enforcement

Local Environmental Health Officers (EHOs) are responsible for enforcing health and safety in hotels, guest houses, bed and breakfasts, holiday homes and caravan sites.

Further guidance

- The Health and Safety Executive produce INDG449 , *Health and Safety made Simple – The Basics for Your Business*, which can be downloaded from their website **www.hse.gov.uk**
- Contact the environmental health department of your local authority for further assistance.

Health and Safety Liabilities

KEY FACTS

- If you are the owner of serviced or self-catering accommodation with control over your premises, the **Occupiers' Liability Acts 1957 and 1984** apply to you.
- The person who controls the premises (the 'occupier') is liable for the physical safety of everyone who comes onto the premises.
- Under the **Employers' Liability (Compulsory Insurance) Act 1969**, employers must have insurance to cover their liability for any harm suffered by an employee at work.
- Public liability insurance is not compulsory but is strongly recommended for accommodation providers.

Your liability to guests and the public

Under the **Occupiers' Liability Act 1957** and **Occupiers' Liability Act 1984**, the person who controls the premises (the 'occupier') is liable for the physical safety of everyone who comes onto the premises. In some cases, this liability also extends to trespassers and other 'uninvited' guests.

Occupiers have what is known as a 'duty of care' to guests and other visitors, and must make sure that the premises are reasonably safe for the purpose for which guests were invited to use them.

Does this legislation apply to me?
- **Yes:** if you are the owner of serviced or self-catering accommodation with control over your premises.

These Acts create a liability, i.e. you can be sued for compensation. You cannot be prosecuted and fined, sent to jail or receive a criminal record under this legislation, but you could be prosecuted under other legislation if you do not take proper precautions.

What does this mean in practice?

You must make sure that the premises are 'reasonably safe'.
For example, you should ensure:

- floors are not slippery
- passageways are clear
- cables are tucked away
- furniture and wall fixtures are secure
- guests are acquainted with emergency procedures and
  the layout of the premises.

Note: If you have children staying on the premises, you need to make sure the premises are reasonably safe for them, not just for adults.

Duty of care

Your duty of care does not normally extend to parts of your premises that are clearly marked as being out of bounds to guests (such as the kitchens in hotels and B&Bs).

Generally, owners are also liable for accidents caused as a result of the actions of their staff or other guests. For example, if a member of staff leaves a bucket on the stairs and someone trips over it and injures themselves, you may be held responsible.

No matter how many notices you put up to the contrary and whatever your booking conditions may say, the law does not allow you to exclude or restrict your liability for death and injuries to guests arising from your negligence (or that of your staff or agents). However, you can take out insurance to cover your liability.

You will not normally be liable for guests who injure themselves while involved in an activity that is not something a guest might reasonably have been expected to do on the premises, such as abseiling from an upper floor window.

Each guest has a duty to take care of his or her own safety. If the guest's own negligence led to an accident, this would reduce, or could even override, any liability that the owner would otherwise have had.

The transportation of guests

If you transport guests, even if this is only occasionally picking up or dropping someone off at the station, there are three issues that need consideration:

- whether a licence is required
- what insurance is required
- health and safety considerations.

LICENCES & CONSENTS

MARKETING

GUESTS

FOOD & DRINK

HEALTH & SAFETY

STAFF

BUSINESS MANAGEMENT & TAX

FURTHER INFORMATION

Occasional transport

At the lowest level, you do not need a licence for occasional transport if:

- you very occasionally help out a guest by providing a lift
- you do not charge for this, and
- your vehicle has fewer than eight seats.

However, you will need to ensure that you have business insurance for your vehicle as, regardless of the lack of payment from the guest, you are still undertaking a business activity.

You should also undertake a quick health and safety assessment prior to transporting the guest – i.e. is the car roadworthy at the time, has the guest put on a seatbelt and is any luggage stowed safely.

Regular transport

If you are providing a lift for your guests to and from their point of arrival as a regular or standard service, then regardless of whether there is a separate charge for this service, you will require a special operating licence and appropriate vehicle insurance.

In this case you will need a Passenger Service Vehicle (PSV) licence. There are two forms of this licence – restricted and full.

Restricted PSV licence

A restricted licence allows you to operate up to two vehicles that have up to 16 seats, provided that you do not use them as part of a passenger transport business, or you are operating your vehicles as part of your accommodation business and that it is not your main occupation. To gain a licence you will have to provide evidence that you:

- have sufficient money to undertake a passenger service business
- have no convictions
- have a maintenance and safety programme in place for your vehicle
- understand the legislation relating to the maximum hours that you can work driving the vehicle
- have the relevant category of driving licence for the vehicle.

For each vehicle with more than nine seats, you will also need a Certificate of Initial Fitness for the vehicle to prove that the vehicle was properly constructed for the purpose of transporting passengers. You will require this even if you buy the vehicle second-hand.

Separately from the requirements for the PSV licence, you will also need to undertake a written health and safety assessment of the operation and keep this updated.

Full PSV licence
If you wish to operate more than two vehicles or a vehicle of more than 16 seats, you will require a Full or Standard PSV licence. In addition to the requirements for a restricted PSV licence, you will also need a certificate of professional competence.

On-demand transport

If you wish to provide customers with an 'on-demand' service that transports them to wherever they request to go, you will require either a Taxi or Private Hire licence. This is an expensive and time-consuming process requiring, among other things, a Criminal Records Bureau check, a knowledge test of roads and destinations in the area, a medical examination and special insurance.

The costs and stringent requirements associated with this form of licence mean that it is not generally recommended for accommodation providers.

Your liability to employees

Under the **Employers' Liability (Compulsory Insurance) Act 1969**, every employer must have insurance to cover their liability for any bodily injury or disease sustained by an employee (this includes casual or part-time employees) at work. Failure to do this is a criminal offence.

How does this apply to me?

If you are a serviced or self-catering accommodation provider and you employ at least one person, you are required to take out and maintain employers' liability insurance cover with a minimum of £5 million for any one claim (most policies available offer £10 million cover).

You must display a copy of the certificate of insurance at your place(s) of business so that it can be seen and read by all your employees. The policy document, or a copy of it, must also be kept available for inspection by Health and Safety Executive inspectors or Environmental Health officers and, for future reference, all policy documents should be retained permanently.

Have you adequate insurance cover?

If you start offering serviced, self-catering or caravan accommodation, you need to consider whether you have adequate insurance to cover, for example, your potential liability under the Occupiers' and Employers' Liability Acts.

Most household policies will not cover:
- your use of the premises for business purposes
- your legal liability to employees or paying guests
- any theft or damage to your property by guests.

In any event, you should contact your existing insurers as soon as possible.

Public liability insurance

One type of insurance cover you should consider, particularly as the public becomes increasingly claims-conscious, is public liability insurance. This covers your liability to guests and others for injury, loss and damage (e.g. under the Occupiers' Liability Acts).

There is no legal requirement to take out public liability insurance, but it is a requirement for participation in VisitEngland's Quality Assessment Schemes for accommodation. It is strongly recommended that you have this type of cover.

Public liability insurance must not be confused with the employers' liability insurance. It also does not cover loss or damage to proprietors' property.

Taking out insurance

Some insurance brokers have special insurance packages available for accommodation providers that include:
- public liability insurance
- employers' liability insurance
- property and contents insurance.

A broker will be able to advise you on these types of comprehensive packages or about adding extra cover to an existing policy.

Your local destination organisation may be able to recommend local insurance brokers who have specific experience in arranging cover for accommodation providers. Insurance brokers should be registered with and regulated by the Financial Conduct Authority. You can check this on the website **www.fca.org.uk**

Insurance for transporting guests

Ensure that you have adequate insurance cover for your vehicle if you transport guests for any reason. See *The transportation of guests* for more details, page 91.

Further guidance

- If anyone makes a claim against you, you should seek legal advice immediately.
- HSE40 (rev4): *Employers' Liability (Compulsory Insurance) Act 1969*, is available free on the HSE's website **www.hse.gov.uk**
- For Taxi and Hackney Carriage information contact your local authority.

Safety Management

KEY FACTS

- The **Management of Health and Safety at Work Regulations 1999** place general duties and responsibilities on all employers at work.

- Employers must carry out a 'suitable and sufficient' assessment of the health and safety risks to employees and others arising from work activities.

- If you have five or more employees, you must keep a record of any significant findings of the assessment and your health and safety arrangements.

- Employers, the self-employed and those in control of work premises must report certain work-related accidents, diseases and dangerous occurrences.

- Employers must provide first aid equipment and facilities appropriate to the circumstances in the workplace.

Main provisions of the Regulations

The **Management of Health and Safety at Work Regulations 1999** follow on from the general responsibilities outlined in the **Health and Safety at Work Act 1974**, by covering in more detail how an employer should manage health and safety at work in order to avoid accidents and ill-health.

Risk assessment is the key to effective management of health and safety and is a legal requirement. The main requirements relating to an accommodation employer are as follows:

Carry out a risk assessment

Employers must carry out a 'suitable and sufficient' assessment of the health and safety risks to employees at work, and any other people, arising out of work activities. The assessment allows you to identify any extra measures that you need to take.

Doing a risk assessment

A risk assessment is nothing more than a careful examination of what, on your premises, could cause harm to people, so that you can weigh up whether you have taken enough precautions or should do more to prevent harm. You also have to do a risk assessment for fire safety (see the *Fire Safety (General)* section), and it is acceptable to combine the fire risk assessment into the general one. There are five basic steps.

Step 1: Look for the hazards, i.e. anything that can cause harm. For most accommodation premises, the hazards are few and simple but assessing them thoroughly is a necessity. You probably know already if, for example, you have steps that are awkward or kitchen furniture that is unstable. Always consider electricity, gas, carbon monoxide poisoning and falls especially carefully as these are potential causes of serious injury or even death. Do not neglect the garden or grounds.

Step 2: Decide who may be harmed and how, including those especially at risk (see section below).

Step 3: Evaluate the risks – consider in particular:
- how likely a mishap is to happen and
- how serious the consequences might be. The more likely and the more serious the potential accident, the higher the risk and the more you need to do to prevent it. Decide whether the existing precautions are adequate or whether more should be done. The test of whether you should do more is whether it is 'reasonably practicable'(see section below) to carry out the possible additional measure.

Step 4: Record your findings.

Step 5: Review your assessment and revise it if necessary.

You don't need to overcomplicate the process. Check that you have taken what precautions you can to avoid injury. You can probably do the assessment yourself. If you get stuck you can contact your local environmental health officer for further advice, although they cannot do the assessment for you.

Consider those especially at risk

You must take into consideration visitors and members of the public who might be affected by your work. You also need to give special consideration to:
- workers who are young

- workers who are inexperienced or new to the particular job
- trainees doing work experience
- workers who have a disability
- guests who are children, elderly, or disabled.

Members of staff at special risk
If you have members of staff at special risk, any risk assessment and health and safety arrangements need to deal specifically with them.

- **Disabled Staff**: if you have disabled staff you must make sure you undertake a risk assessment that takes into account their impairment and, as well as undertaking any adjustments, that you have systems and emergency procedures in place that do not expose them to undue risk.
- **Staff with poor English**: if you have staff whose first language is not English, you must make sure they understand, for example, all the preventative health and safety measures, signs and emergency procedures.
- **Young people**: there are special requirements covering young people (under the age of 18), which require the employer to do a specific risk assessment and give specific information to the young person and their parents or guardians (see *Employing Children*, page 161).
- **New and expectant mothers**: again there are special requirements and considerations that are explained in an HSE guide *New and expectant mothers who work*– see *Further guidance* below.

Reasonably practicable
This is a balance between the cost and inconvenience on the one hand, and the benefit of the safety improvement on the other.

For example, if the cost of repairing a loose carpet is small, and the risk is tripping, falling down stairs and breaking bones, then you **must** make the repair. At the other extreme if the removal of an awkward step would involve rebuilding part of the house, and the consequences of any foreseeable trip are minor, it wouldn't be reasonably practicable to do it (although of course warnings might well be needed).

Health and safety arrangements
You must put into place any extra measures identified in the assessment, along with arrangements for:
- organising health and safety in the workplace
- ensuring safety procedures are followed
- reviewing and updating the measures and procedures.

Health surveillance

Employers must provide health surveillance for employees, appropriate to the risks identified in the assessment.

Competent person

Employers must appoint a competent person, preferably a member of staff with the necessary training or experience, to assist in health and safety matters.

Recording

If you have five or more employees, you must keep a record of:

- any 'significant findings' of your assessment
- your health and safety arrangements (best included in your overall 'health and safety policy statement' – a template form for you to use is available on the HSE website **www.hse.gov.uk/simple-health-safety/write.htm**).

Even if you have fewer than five employees, it is still sensible to keep a record. This will give you increased protection if there is an accident.

Emergency procedures

Employers must draw up procedures for dealing with emergencies and establishing contact with the emergency services (such as fire and medical care).

Information, instruction and training

You must give your employees information on the risks, the preventative measures and the emergency procedures so they can understand them.

You need to consult with your employees on these and any other key health and safety issues.

You also need to make sure that when a new employee starts you give them sufficient health and safety training so they can go about their work safely. For example, if you have a new cleaner starting, you need to explain how to use all the different cleaning agents safely.

The staff training needs to be repeated or updated as appropriate; it should take place during working hours and must not be paid for by employees.

Agency workers

If you hire agency workers, you must tell the employment agency about:

- risks to the worker's health and safety and steps you have taken to control them

UPDATED

LICENCES & CONSENTS

MARKETING

GUESTS

FOOD & DRINK

HEALTH & SAFETY

STAFF

BUSINESS MANAGEMENT & TAX

FURTHER INFORMATION

- any necessary legal or professional qualifications or skills
- any necessary health surveillance.

Temporary staff

Employers must give temporary staff information, before they start, on any special qualifications or skills required to do the work safely, and any health surveillance you are required to provide.

Employees' duties

Employees have a duty to follow health and safety instructions and to report dangers.

Accident reporting

If you are an employer, self-employed or in control of work premises, you are required by law to report certain work-related accidents, diseases and dangerous occurrences. Details of the types of accidents that you need to report can be found at the RIDDOR website **www.hse.gov.uk/riddor** (see *Further guidance* section below).

All incidents can be reported online (**www.hse.gov.uk/riddor/ report.htm**) but a telephone service remains for reporting fatal and major injuries only – call the Incident Contact Centre on 0845 300 9923.

You will be sent a copy of the final report for your own records – this meets your statutory obligation to keep records of all reportable incidents for inspection and also allows you to correct any error or omission.

First aid

Employers must provide first-aid equipment and facilities appropriate to the circumstances in the workplace. The minimum would be a suitably stocked first-aid box and a person appointed to take charge of first-aid arrangements.

First-aid provision should be part of your risk assessment process under the Management of Health and Safety at Work Regulations (see *Carry out a risk assessment* section above).

You have no responsibility for administering first aid to guests or the public at large, although you should be familiar with local medical facilities.

Other Regulations

Other health and safety legislation supplements these general responsibilities with specific requirements. The key Regulations are covered in this service – see the following sections:

- *Fire Safety (General)* see page 125
- *Fire Safety of Furniture and Furnishings* see page 133
- *Hazards in the Workplace* see page 108
- *Hazards from Work Activities* see page 102
- *Swimming, Gym and Outdoor Safety* see page 121.

Further guidance

The Health and Safety Executive has developed a website **Health and Safety Made Simple www.hse.gov.uk/simple-health-safety/index.htm** dedicated to providing small businesses with straightforward advice and information on health and safety issues. This provides basic information on the issues in this section.

For more detailed information, a wide range of guidance and information on health and safety issues is available online through the Health and Safety Executive website **www.hse.gov.uk** including:

Managing safety:
- INDG275: *Plan, Do, Check, Act - An introduction to managing for health and safety*
- INDG163: *Five Steps to Risk Assessment*

For the catering industry:
- There are a range of guidance publications for the catering industry on a dedicated HSE web page **www.hse.gov.uk/catering/guidance.htm**

People especially at risk:
- CAIS19: *Health and Safety of New and Expectant Mothers in the Catering Industry*
- CAIS21: *Health and Safety of Children and Young People in Catering*

First aid and accident reporting:
- RIDDOR – **www.hse.gov.uk/riddor/report.htm**
- INDG347: *Basic Advice on First Aid at Work*

LICENCES & CONSENTS

MARKETING

GUESTS

FOOD & DRINK

HEALTH & SAFETY

STAFF

BUSINESS MANAGEMENT & TAX

FURTHER INFORMATION

Hazards from Work Activities

KEY FACTS

● All employers must consider the risks to staff arising from the hazards associated with work activities. A hazard is something with the potential to cause harm.

● Any work equipment must be suitable for the job and safe, as required by the **Provision and Use of Work Equipment Regulations 1998**.

● If staff habitually use computers or other kinds of display screen equipment, the **Health and Safety (Display Screen Equipment) Regulations 1992** apply.

● If staff lift and carry objects, the **Manual Handling Operations Regulations 1992** (as amended) apply.

● Under the **Work at Height Regulations 2005**, employers are required to avoid work at height where possible, or, where it cannot be avoided, to take measures to ensure that the person working at height does not fall.

● If you are an employer you must assess all hazardous substances.

● These are the main regulations to be aware of, but other health and safety legislation may apply, depending on the work activity being done.

Work equipment

The **Provision and Use of Work Equipment Regulations 1998** cover the safety of work equipment (including an employee's own equipment and equipment used by a self-employed person, e.g. a cleaner who cleans your self-catering accommodation from time to time).

The general duties that are of particular relevance to an accommodation employer are:

● to make sure that equipment is suitable – select the right equipment for the job

- to make sure equipment is properly installed and safe to operate
- to give proper training and instructions on the use of the equipment and follow manufacturers' or suppliers' instructions
- to make sure equipment is maintained and in good repair through regular maintenance, inspection and, if appropriate, thorough examination
- to provide equipment which conforms to EC product safety directives.

Display screens

The **Health and Safety (Display Screen Equipment) Regulations 1992** apply where staff habitually use computers or other kinds of display screen equipment (also known as visual display units or VDUs) as part of their normal work.

Employers have to:
- analyse workstations, and assess and reduce risks
- ensure workstations meet minimum requirements set out in the Regulations
- plan VDU work so that staff have breaks or changes of activity
- provide eye and eyesight tests for VDU users who request them, and provide spectacles if special ones are needed
- provide health and safety training and information for VDU users.

Safe manual handling

More than a third of all 'over three day' injuries reported each year to the HSE and local authorities are the result of manual handling. In the catering industry alone it is the second most common cause of injury.

As seen in the *Safety Management* section (page 96), the **Management of Health and Safety at Work Regulations 1999** require an employer to assess the risks in any work activity and take the appropriate precautions.

In addition, the **Manual Handling Operations Regulations 1992** require an employer to:
- ensure, so far as it is reasonably practicable, that employees are not required to undertake any manual handling operations at work if there is a risk of them being injured
- if any hazardous operations cannot be avoided, thoroughly assess the risks, and take steps to minimise the risks of injury as far as reasonably practicable.

Work at height

Falls from a height account for 40 to 60 fatalities and about 4,000 injuries every year. One of the main causes is falls from ladders.

The Regulations and types of work at height

Work at height means working where a person could fall and be injured. It therefore includes working at ground level next to a well or cellar opening, etc. There is no fixed height that is considered dangerous. This depends partly on where the person might fall (e.g. on grass or concrete).

The **Work at Height Regulations 2005** require employers to avoid work at height where possible, or, where it cannot be avoided, to take measures to ensure that the person working at height does not fall. There must be a risk assessment carried out before a person works at a height.

Light work of short duration may be carried out using ladders if conditions are suitable and there are adequate hand-holds and the ladder can be secured.

People involved in working at a height must be competent and adequately trained and supervised.

You must:
- avoid work at height if you can
- use equipment or take other measures to prevent a fall if you can't avoid work at height
- as a last resort, if no more can be done to prevent a fall, take measures to minimise the consequences of a fall.

Window cleaning and painting are common reasons for working at height. Although very common, window cleaning using ladders has led to many deaths in the past. A ladder is not usually a safe way to clean first floor windows and above. If you decide to have work done by a person standing on a ladder, you must ensure you have measures in place to prevent him or her from falling off, or the ladder from slipping. There are alternatives, such as:
- water-fed hose cleaning
- the installation of interior eye bolts by a specialist company, that enables windows to be cleaned using a harness.

Things to consider

To ascertain the risk of falling from height, consider these questions:
- how far would a person fall?
- are there adequate hand-holds?

- are there any fragile surfaces (e.g. roof lights) involved?
- where might the person land? (e.g. on grass, concrete, spiked railings)
- what is the nature of the work to be done (consider especially any leaning, stretching, or carrying that might increase the risk of falling)
- is the ladder or other equipment secured, top and bottom, to prevent it slipping?

Falling off a ladder carries a significant risk of severe injury or death. Ladders are best regarded as a means of access and not as a place from which to do work.

Reducing risks from working at height

To help prevent falls from a height you should assess and reduce the risks to all your workers and ensure they are:
- trained and have suitable and safe equipment for the task(s)
- properly managed and supervised
- provided with sufficient protection measures (e.g. suitable and sufficient personal protective equipment) while they are working at height.

Hazardous substances

Hazardous substances can generally be identified from the product label. In most accommodation, only domestic cleaning materials will be used, but some products used for drain cleaning, rodent control, gardening, or other purposes may also be hazardous.

COSHH assessment

If you are an employer you must assess all hazardous substances under the **Control of Substances Hazardous to Health Regulations 2002** (COSHH). The employer has a duty to remove employees' exposure to hazardous substances, e.g. powerful commercial cleaning agents or, where this is not possible, to adequately control it.

To help with the assessment, you may need to obtain a safety data sheet (SDS) from the supplier or manufacturer of the hazardous substance. (This will not be necessary for very common products like household bleach, for which plenty of information is readily available.) The SDS describes the substance and the dangers it may pose. You will only then be in a position to plan the measures that you will need to take to control the substance and prevent harm. It will usually be best to keep it in a secure location especially if there are children on the premises.

LICENCES & CONSENTS

MARKETING

GUESTS

FOOD & DRINK

HEALTH & SAFETY

STAFF

BUSINESS MANAGEMENT & TAX

FURTHER INFORMATION

COSHH Essentials

By logging on to COSHH Essentials on the Health and Safety Executive website **www.hse.gov.uk/coshh/essentials/index.htm** you can carry out a FREE, quick and simple risk assessment (COSHH Essentials is also available in a paper version which you can buy from HSE Books). You will need to enter some very basic information about the chemicals or products that you use and the system will automatically work out the correct control procedures for you. Alternatively, for some tasks such as cleaning, you can simply go directly to the control advice.

Other legislation

The Regulations already mentioned are the main ones to be aware of, but other health and safety legislation may apply, depending on the work activity.

Further guidance

The Health and Safety Executive provides a wide range of guidance material on health and safety legislation and how to comply with it. These publications can be downloaded from the HSE website **www.hse.gov.uk** and include:

General Guidance:
- INDG291: *Providing and using work equipment safely*

Display screens:
- L26: *Work with display screen equipment*
- INDG36 (rev4): *Working with Display Screen Equipment: A brief guide*

Safe manual handling:
- CAIS24: *Preventing back pain and other aches and pains to kitchen and food service staff*
- **www.hse.gov.uk/msd** provides up-to-date information on health and safety relating to musculoskeletal disorders which is the general name for conditions such as back pain and repetitive strain injury (RSI). It also includes the online Manual Handling Assessment Chart (MAC) tool.

Working from height:
- INDG401: *Work at Height Regulations 2005 – A Brief Guide*
- INDG402: *Safe Use of Ladders and Stepladders – An Employer's Guide*
- INDG 290: *Lifting Equipment at Work*

Hazardous substances:
- INDG136: *Working with Substances Hazardous to Health*
- *COSHH Essentials, easy steps to control chemicals* can be viewed at **www.hse.gov.uk/coshh/essentials/index.htm**

LICENCES & CONSENTS

MARKETING

GUESTS

FOOD & DRINK

HEALTH & SAFETY

STAFF

BUSINESS MANAGEMENT & TAX

FURTHER INFORMATION

LICENCES & CONSENTS

MARKETING

GUESTS

FOOD & DRINK

HEALTH & SAFETY

STAFF

BUSINESS MANAGEMENT & TAX

FURTHER INFORMATION

Hazards in the Workplace

KEY FACTS

- All employers must consider the risks to staff arising from the hazards associated with aspects of the workplace. A hazard is something with the potential to cause harm.

- The working environment must be suitable, at a reasonable temperature, have adequate lighting and ventilation, and include sufficient rest facilities.

- Employers should reduce the risk of slips, trips and falls by cleaning spillages, keeping walkways clear and organising work better.

- All electrical systems in places of work must be maintained 'so far as is reasonably practicable' to avoid danger to all who use the premises (including guests).

- Although Health and Safety can be a complex area of legislation, there are two main sets of regulations that you need to be aware of: the **Workplace (Health, Safety and Welfare) Regulations 1992** and the **Management of Health and Safety at Work Regulations 1999**.

The Workplace (Health, Safety and Welfare) Regulations 1992

The **Workplace (Health, Safety and Welfare) Regulations 1992** cover your employees' working environment, setting out the requirements in respect of:

- the quality of the working environment (e.g. reasonable temperature, lighting and ventilation)
- suitability of the environment (e.g. room dimensions, space, passageways and windows)
- the facilities for your employees (e.g. toilets, washing and eating facilities, drinking water, changing and rest areas, and rest facilities for pregnant women)
- the maintenance and cleanliness of the workplace, equipment and facilities.

The Management of Health and Safety at Work Regulations 1999

The main requirement of the **Management of Health and Safety at Work Regulations 1999** is that employers must carry out risk assessments to eliminate or reduce risks. Employers with five or more employees need to record the significant findings of a risk assessment – it is not necessary to record risk assessments for trivial or insignificant risks. In addition, employers also need to:

- make arrangements for implementing the health and safety measures identified as necessary by risk assessments
- monitor and review those arrangements
- appoint people with sufficient knowledge, skills, experience and training to help them to implement these arrangements
- set up emergency procedures and provide information about them to employees
- provide clear information, supervision and training for employees and ensure that suitably competent people are appointed who are capable of carrying out the tasks entrusted to them
- work together with any other employer(s) operating from the same workplace, sharing information on the risks that other staff may be exposed to, e.g. cleaning, catering or maintenance contractors
- take particular account of risks to new and expectant mothers.

Use of safety glass

The **Workplace (Health, Safety and Welfare) Regulations 1992** include the use of safety glass or materials in the workplace.

These regulations will not normally apply to self-catering accommodation unless someone works there, e.g. a cleaner. However, the **General Product Safety Regulations 2005** could potentially be applied to self-catering businesses (see the *Product Safety* section, page 114) and could be taken to cover glass in doors, windows and elsewhere. Always be sure that the glass in your property is adequate for the use to which it is being put.

If there is a large pane of glass, especially if it extends to below waist height, you need to consider the risk of it being broken or walked into. If the circumstances lead to the conclusion that there is no risk, no action need be taken, but if there is a risk of it being broken it should be glazed with safety glass and also marked so that it is obviously present (e.g. with an etched design).

What glass is covered by the Regulations?

It is not the case that the Regulations apply to all glazing. In the past, a number of glaziers have misrepresented these Regulations in attempts to persuade businesses to replace or modify all windows, glazed doors, walls or partitions. The actual requirement is as follows.

Windows and transparent or translucent doors, gates and walls
Every window or other transparent or translucent surface in a wall or partition, and every transparent or translucent surface in a door or gate shall, where necessary for reasons of health or safety:

- be of safety material or be protected against breakage of the transparent or translucent material
- be appropriately marked or incorporate features so as, in either case, to make it apparent.

General guidance to the Regulations then adds that transparent or translucent surfaces in doors, gates, walls and partitions should be of a safety material or be adequately protected against breakage in the following cases:

- in doors and gates, and door and gate side panels, where any part of the transparent or translucent surface is at shoulder level or below
- in windows, walls and partitions, where any part of the transparent or translucent surface is at waist level or below, except in glasshouses where people will be likely to be aware of the presence of glazing and avoid contact.

It is clear that safety glass or materials are only necessary in certain cases where a particular need or risk has been identified. Indeed, the chances are that it will already have been fitted as a matter of routine. Wholesale replacement of windows and glazed doors or partitions is not implied by the Regulations.

Slips and trips

Accidents as a result of a slip or trip are the most common cause of injuries at work. Resulting falls can be serious. They can happen in all kinds of businesses, but sectors such as the food and catering industry report higher than average numbers of incidents and it is a particularly important subject if members of the public use your premises.

What are the chances of slips and trips at your workplace?

To identify problems and prevent accidents happening, consider the following questions:

- do you have floors that are, or can become slippery, e.g. when wet?

- does spillage or contamination occur and is it dealt with quickly?
- do people use unlit areas such as paths or yards in the dark?
- might temporary work such as maintenance or alterations take place? It could introduce slipping and tripping hazards such as trailing cables
- do you use floor-cleaning materials anywhere?
- are the right methods and materials being used?

Reducing risk

Effective solutions are often simple, cheap and lead to other benefits. You should ensure that you:

- clean up spillages, organise work better and keep walkways clear
- 'design-in' safety equipment and materials
- obtain help and advice, e.g. from the Health and Safety Executive, publications and guidance, or your local environmental health officer.

Electricity at work

The **Electricity at Work Regulations 1989** are wide-ranging. Accommodation employers should be aware of one objective in particular, that all electrical systems in places of work must be maintained 'so far as is reasonably practicable' to avoid danger to all who use the premises (including guests).

These regulations only apply to self-catering accommodation if you have one or more employees working on the premises. Of course your general duties under the HSW Act include ensuring that guests are protected from electrical hazards and these still apply to self-catering.

The safety of electrical equipment in self-catering accommodation is also covered in the *Product Safety* section, see page 114.

Which electrical equipment is affected?

All electrical systems are covered by the regulations, whether they are used solely by:

- you and your staff
- you, your staff and guests
- your guests.

'Electrical systems' means the mains wiring and all mains-powered electric equipment.

Electrical equipment brought in by guests is not affected by these Regulations, which are restricted to matters within your control.

Testing and maintenance

There is no specific requirement for the regular routine testing of systems. Nevertheless, you do have a duty of maintenance under the Regulations and regular testing is the only practical way for you to be sure that you are complying with this duty.

- The **fixed wiring installation** should be tested every few years – exactly how often will depend on its age and the likelihood that it has been damaged. It is important to remember that while there are no specific rules requiring testing every so often, if you never have it tested you will probably not be carrying out your general duties to ensure the safety of your guests.

- You will often be able to tell from a quick visual inspection whether a piece of **portable equipment** is faulty or damaged. Regular visual inspection is the most important measure you can take. This will detect a large proportion of common faults such as damaged plugs, frayed or damaged cables, or cracks in a casing.

If you wish to have your electrical systems tested professionally, you should ensure that those doing the work are competent. This can be done by using electrical contractors who belong to either the Electrical Contractors' Association or to the National Inspection Council for Electrical Installation Contracting (NICEIC). However, portable appliance testing can be carried out by a trained, competent person who need not be a qualified electrician.

Records of testing and maintenance

Keep a record of all the testing and maintenance that has been carried out. In the event of an accident involving the electrical systems on your premises, this record should enable you to demonstrate that you have complied with your duty of maintenance under the regulations.

Cold callers

Health and Safety legislation is an area that has been targeted by disreputable firms trying to sell products and services. Do not be intimidated by sales people who may be misrepresenting the Regulations in an attempt to win your custom. Remember, in particular, that the Regulations do not generally specify what materials you must use, what tests you should undertake or how often you should undertake them.

Further guidance

HSE priced and free publications are available by mail order from
HSE Books **www.hse.gov.uk**.

Work environment:
- INDG224 (Rev2): *Workplace Health, Safety and Welfare:
  A Short Guide for Managers*
- INDG293: *Welfare at Work: Guidance for Employers on
  Welfare Provisions*

Slips and trips:
- INDG225 (Rev2): *Preventing Slips and Trips at Work*
- INDG244: *Workplace Health, Safety and Welfare*
- HSG155: *Slips and Trips: Guidance for Employers on Identifying
  and Controlling Risks*, £7.50

Electricity at work:
- INDG236: *Maintaining Portable Electrical Equipment in Low-risk
  Environments*
- INDG231: *Electrical Safety and You*

LICENCES & CONSENTS

MARKETING

GUESTS

FOOD & DRINK

HEALTH & SAFETY

STAFF

BUSINESS MANAGEMENT & TAX

FURTHER INFORMATION

Product Safety

KEY FACTS

- Operators of accommodation premises have a responsibility for ensuring that gas appliances and flues in the premises are safely maintained and checked. All safety checks must be carried out by a Gas Safe registered engineer.

- Electrical equipment safety regulations require that all electrical equipment supplied 'in the course of business' is safe. There is no specific requirement for annual maintenance, but to ensure electrical equipment remains safe, you are strongly advised to have it checked and serviced regularly by a registered electrician.

- The general product safety regulations apply if you provide self-catering accommodation. The essential requirements are to ensure that you supply only safe products to your guests, and to ensure that a product remains safe throughout its period of use.

Gas safety

Installing and maintaining gas appliances

Each year there are fatalities from carbon monoxide poisoning caused by poorly installed or badly maintained gas appliances and flues. There are also proven complaints from guests about the safety of gas appliances in their accommodation premises, normally self-catering. The **Gas Safety (Installation and Use) Regulations 1998** are there to protect you and your guests.

They supplement any responsibilities you may have under the **Health and Safety at Work, etc Act 1974** and the **Management of Health and Safety at Work Regulations 1999** .

Registration schemes for gas engineers

The CORGI registration scheme for gas engineers was ended on 1 April 2009 and has been replaced by the *Gas Safe* registration scheme. It is illegal for any engineer to undertake work under the

Gas Safety (Installation and Use) Regulations 1998 unless they are *Gas Safe* registered.

What do the gas safety regulations cover?

- The Regulations specifically deal with the installation, maintenance and use of gas appliances, fittings and flues in domestic, residential and commercial premises.
- The Regulations place duties on a wide range of people including gas suppliers and those installing and working on gas equipment.
- The Regulations include extensive duties on accommodation providers for ensuring appliances and flues in the premises they let are safely maintained and checked.

What types of premises are affected?

The premises affected include all accommodation:

- self-catering properties
- hotels
- hostels
- guest houses
- bed and breakfasts
- permanently sited caravans
- touring caravans and inland waterway boats hired out in the course of business
- privately owned inland waterway boats used privately for domestic or residential purposes
- commercial installations generally.

What are my main duties?

You are required to:

- ensure all gas fittings and flues are maintained in a safe condition
- ensure an **annual safety check** is carried out on each gas appliance/flue by a Gas Safe registered engineer (see *Registration schemes for gas engineers* above for more details)
- keep a written record of the inspection for two years, containing information such as the following:
  - the date of the check
  - location and details of the appliance/flue
  - any defects found and action taken
  - a confirmation that the check was made in accordance with the Regulations.
- issue a copy of the record to any person staying for more than 28 days, or if the premises is let for 28 days or less, display a copy of the record prominently in the premises.

Duties as an employer

You have a duty to ensure that the gas appliances under your control are 'maintained in a safe condition so as to prevent injury to any person'. This includes staff or people that you contract to work on your premises (e.g. cleaners).

Other important provisions

Other important provisions include the following:

- anyone carrying out work on gas appliances or fittings not as part of their business (e.g. as a favour to you) must still be competent (do-it-yourself work can be dangerous and illegal)

Note: employers can only use Gas Safe engineers (see *Registration schemes for gas engineers* for more details).

- you must not use any gas appliance or fitting you know or suspect to be unsafe
- with the exception of 'room-sealed' appliances, there are restrictions on the installation of gas appliances in sleeping areas fitted after 1 January 1996
- it is illegal to install instantaneous water heaters that are not room-sealed or fitted with a safety device which automatically turns off the gas supply before a dangerous level of poisonous fumes builds up.

Additional precautions

The Health and Safety Executive highlights additional precautions:

- whenever draught exclusion, double glazing or a conservatory extension is fitted to a room containing a gas appliance, the appliance should subsequently be checked for safety
- never block or obstruct any fixed ventilation grilles or air bricks
- never block or cover outside flues.

While there is no legal requirement to install a carbon monoxide detector, their use is now a requirement of the VisitEngland accommodation grading scheme and is considered best practice for properties which have a gas supply.

Your liability and your agent's

Important: If you use an agent to manage your properties (e.g. self-catering accommodation), you should ensure that the management contract specifies who is responsible for the maintenance of gas appliances and for keeping records to indicate when this maintenance has been carried out.

The liability of purely marketing and booking agencies (rather than managing agencies) under these Regulations is unclear. Some

UPDATED

agencies therefore seek to exclude themselves from liability by inserting into their contracts with owners a clause which commits those owners to ensuring that their property complies at all times with the gas safety requirements.

Electrical equipment

What do the Regulations cover?
The **Electrical Equipment (Safety) Regulations 1994** require, among other things, that all electrical equipment supplied 'in the course of business' is safe. This applies equally to new and second-hand equipment.

Do the Regulations apply to me?
The Regulations apply to everyone who supplies electrical equipment in the course of their business, regardless of whether or not their business is actually the supply of electrical equipment. The Regulations are particularly relevant to self-catering accommodation, as equipment in these premises may not be covered by the Electricity at Work Regulations (see the *Hazards in the Workplace* section for more details).

What does safe mean?
For electrical equipment to be regarded as safe, there should be no risk (or only a minimal risk) that the equipment will in any way cause death or injury to any person or domestic animal, or cause damage to property.

If you are buying any new electrical equipment in the UK, it should be 'safe' as manufacturers and suppliers are bound by the same Regulations. It should also carry a CE marking (indicating that the manufacturer believes the product complies with all relevant European Directives and safety standards). If you are buying second-hand electrical equipment from a professional dealer (or auction house) it should likewise be 'safe', although it does not have to carry a CE marking.

Do I need to maintain electrical equipment?
Although these Regulations require electrical equipment to be safe, unlike for gas appliances there is no specific requirement for annual maintenance. However, to be sure that the electrical equipment in your accommodation remains safe, you are strongly advised to have it checked and serviced regularly by a registered electrician.

The Health and Safety Executive (HSE) provides a free guidance publication *Electrical Safety and You* which you can download from their website **http://www.hse.gov.uk/pubns/indg231.pdf**. This provides useful information about checking electrical equipment.

Note: letting agents can also be held responsible for the safety of the electrical equipment in accommodation they let, depending on the terms of their agreements with property owners. Check your agreement and speak with your agent to ensure you both understand who is responsible for the safety of electrical products.

General product safety

The **General Product Safety Regulations 2005** are aimed at making sure that all goods supplied to consumers (new or second-hand) are safe.

The 2005 Regulations cover products made available to consumers for their use in the course of a delivery of a service (e.g. the provision of a hairdryer in a hotel room or self-catering cottage for the guest's own use).

Where a product is already subject to other existing regulations then those regulations will still apply to that product. The General Product Safety Regulations will also apply where they go further than the existing Regulations.

Do the Regulations apply to me?
Yes: if you are providing self-catering accommodation.

Note: letting agents can be held responsible for product safety in the accommodation, depending on the terms of their agreement with the property owners.

How do I comply with the Regulations?
The essential requirements are to ensure that you supply only safe products to your guests, and undertake relevant activities (where appropriate) to help ensure that a product remains safe throughout its period of use.

A safe product is defined as 'any product which under normal or reasonably foreseeable conditions of use presents no risk or only the minimum risk compatible with the product's use and which is consistent with a high level of protection for consumers'.

You are required to provide guests with all relevant information, warnings and instructions for the safe operation and use of products. You are also required to keep yourself informed about possible risks.

General precautions

The Regulations require no formal testing and as you can see from the examples below, it is really just a matter of common sense and routine checking.

- If instructions are needed to operate a piece of household equipment, make sure that they are provided.
- If a piece of equipment provided is damaged, repair it, e.g. an ironing board with loose or fragile legs.
- If an item of furniture or equipment can be damaged and made dangerous by children playing with it, make sure your guests know this.

Requirements as a 'distributor' of products

As a 'distributor' of products, you are also required, 'within the limits of your activity', to participate in monitoring the safety of products that you supply and to pass on information on product risks. In practice this means:

- passing on to guests information provided by producers about product risks
- passing back to producers safety complaints, information and experiences on safety-related matters obtained from guests
- co-operating with the authorities and others in the supply chain in taking action to avoid or remove those risks.

Note: if you discover that you have provided an unsafe product for your guests to use, you are now obliged to notify your local authority of the fact and what action you have taken to remove the risks to your guests.

Enforcement

The Trading Standards department of your local authority is responsible for enforcing the Regulations mentioned above (except for the Electrical Equipment Regulations).

Further guidance

Gas safety:

- Gas safety advice line – set up by the Health and Safety Executive to offer telephone advice on gas safety matters. Ring freephone 0800 300 363. (The lines are open 08:00 -17:30 hrs Monday to Thursday and 08:00 –17:00 hrs on Friday).
- For further information on the Gas Safe Register visit **www.gassaferegister.co.uk**

LICENCES & CONSENTS

MARKETING

GUESTS

FOOD & DRINK

HEALTH & SAFETY

STAFF

BUSINESS MANAGEMENT & TAX

FURTHER INFORMATION

- There is a range of guidance publications available on the HSE website **www.hse.gov.uk/gas/domestic/links.htm** including:
  - INDG238: *Gas Appliances. Get Them Checked, Keep Them Safe*
  - INDG285: *Landlords, A Guide to Landlords' Duties: Gas Safety (Installation and Use) Regulations 1998.*

Electrical equipment safety:
- INDG231: *Electricity and You* can be downloaded from the HSE website **www.hse.gov.uk**
- Further advice is available from the Health and Safety Executive who are responsible for enforcing the Electrical Equipment Regulations.

General:
- Further advice is available from the Trading Standards Department of your local authority who enforce the Regulations mentioned above (except for the Electrical Equipment Regulations).
- A copy of a Department of Trade and Industry (DTI) guidance publication *General Product Safety Regulations 2005* can be downloaded from **www.berr.gov.uk/files/file22713.pdf**.

Swimming, Gym and Outdoor Safety

KEY FACTS

- There are no specific regulations on swimming pool or gym safety, but you must manage these activities so they comply with health and safety legislation.
- Anyone who sells adventure activities intended for young people under 18 must be inspected and licensed under the **Adventure Activities Licensing Regulations 2004**.

Swimming and gym safety

Drownings in swimming pools in the UK are rare, with only one fatality last year. However, this does not mean that you should not pay particular attention to the safety of guests and staff around pool areas.

General legislation that applies

Currently there is no specific legislation on swimming pool or gym safety. These are covered by general health and safety regulations. Your main responsibility as a pool or gym operator, in relation to the safety of your guests or clients, is to be found in the **Health and Safety at Work, etc Act 1974** and the **Management of Health and Safety at Work Regulations 1999**. See the sections on the *Health and Safety at Work Act* and *Safety Management* for more information.

Safety in swimming pools is a complex subject and should be studied closely by those who manage them. A thorough risk assessment should be carried out, and amongst other things this will determine whether constant supervision is needed. This risk assessment should include topics such as:
- slipping and tripping
- signage
- water depth and any changes of level

- water clarity
- the availability of alcohol or likelihood of swimming after drinking
- child protection issues
- unsupervised children
- hazards in changing areas
- life-saving equipment
- rescue and emergency arrangements.

Guidance on swimming pools

The Health and Safety Executive (HSE) has published a very useful guide, *Managing Health and Safety in Swimming Pools*, which provides detailed guidance on the risks associated with swimming pool operation and the precautions which may be taken to help achieve a safer environment. It also covers supervision and signage.

The guide draws on legislation from the **Health and Safety at Work, etc Act 1974**, the **Management of Health and Safety at Work Regulations 1999**, the **Workplace Health and Safety Regulations 1992** and the **Provision and Use of Work Equipment Regulations 1998**.

Outdoor activity safety measures

Anyone who sells adventure activities intended for young people under 18 must be inspected and licensed under the **Adventure Activities Licensing Regulations 2004**.

Do I need an inspection and licence?

Yes: if you provide, in return for payment, any of the activities listed below to young people under 18 unaccompanied by a parent or guardian.

Activities covered by the inspection and licensing scheme

The scheme covers 26 main activities under the following four specified adventure activity groups:

- **caving:** underground exploration in natural caves and mines including pot-holing, cave diving and mine exploration.
- **climbing:** climbing, traversing, abseiling and scrambling activities, except on purpose-designed climbing walls or abseiling towers.
- **trekking:** walking, running, pony trekking, mountain biking, off-piste skiing, and related activities when done in moor or mountain country which is remote (i.e. over 30 minutes travelling time from the nearest road or refuge).
- **water sports:** canoeing, rafting, sailing and related activities when done on tidal or inland waters which are more than 100 metres across or are turbulent.

The scheme does not cover:
- activities that are offered to young people who are accompanied by their parents or guardians
- activities offered by voluntary associations to their members or by schools to their pupils.

Note: The Health and Safety Executive is currently looking to abolish the licensing scheme for the four specified adventure activities and to replace it with a series of 'Codes of Practice'. However, as yet, no decision has been made and operators are still required to obtain a licence.

The activity provider's duty under the Regulations

The primary duty of the activity provider is to ensure the safety of young people using activity facilities. To be able to comply with this duty, providers must have in place a safety management system that involves a systematic approach to recognising risks and making sure something is done to control them.

Important factors include:
- the risk assessment process
- the number of competent instructors
- the suitability and maintenance of equipment
- emergency procedures.

The inspection/licence process

The HSE took over responsibility for the Adventure Activities Licensing Authority (AALA) on 1 April 2007 and has enforcement responsibility for the 2004 Regulations.

All the inspections and most of the administration work that the AALA carried out have been taken over by Tourism Quality Services Ltd (TQS) under contract. TQS is operating under the name Adventure Activities Licensing Service (AALS).

Applications, inspections and licensing are handled by TQS. Inspections are rigorous. Licences will only be granted if the licensing authority is satisfied that the applicant meets management safety requirements.

Further guidance

- The publication *Managing Health and Safety in Swimming Pools* can be purchased on the HSE website
  www.hse.gov.uk/entertainment/leisure/swimming-pool.htm
- Health and safety standards for private pools are enforced by the environmental health department of your local authority.

- Information on Adventure Activities and the change from licensing to Codes of Practice is available on the HSE website **www.hse.gov.uk/aala**.

LICENCES & CONSENTS

MARKETING

GUESTS

FOOD & DRINK

HEALTH & SAFETY

STAFF

BUSINESS MANAGEMENT & TAX

FURTHER INFORMATION

Fire Safety (General)

LICENCES & CONSENTS

MARKETING

GUESTS

FOOD & DRINK

HEALTH & SAFETY

STAFF

BUSINESS MANAGEMENT & TAX

FURTHER INFORMATION

KEY FACTS

- Fire safety legislation applies to virtually all workplaces including hotels, B&Bs and self-catering properties.

- A 'suitable and sufficient' fire risk assessment must be carried out, and where there are five or more employees, the assessment should be recorded.

- There should be one person responsible for the fire risk assessment and ensuring that fire protection and prevention measures are observed and maintained.

- An emergency plan should be drawn up. It should be displayed in the form of a fire action notice in guest rooms and adjacent to the fire alarm call points in the staff and common areas.

Fire safety

On 1 October 2006 there was a major change in UK fire safety legislation with the introduction of the **Regulatory Reform (Fire Safety) Order 2005**. This requires the 'responsible person' in virtually all workplaces, including hotels, B&Bs and self-catering properties, to adopt a self-assessment approach to fire safety in the workplace.

The **Regulatory Reform (Fire Safety) Order 2005** applies to England and Wales, but there is equivalent legislation in Scotland and Northern Ireland.

- In Scotland the **Fire (Scotland) Act 2005** and the **Fire Safety (Scotland) Regulations 2006** apply.
- In Northern Ireland the relevant legislation is the **Fire and Rescue Services (Northern Ireland) Order 2006**.

Do the Regulations apply to me?

Yes: the Regulations apply to all accommodation premises, including self-catering accommodation.

The key requirement is that a 'suitable and sufficient' fire risk assessment must be carried out.

If you have **five or more employees** the fire risk assessment should be recorded. However, we strongly recommend that even if you do not employ five or more people, you should **keep a record** in case any issues arise concerning your fire safety provisions. A record will also prove that you have undertaken an assessment.

Note: it is also a requirement of VisitEngland's Quality Assessment Scheme that you demonstrate to the assessor that you have carried out your assessment. In addition, your public liability insurance provider will require proof that you have undertaken an assessment.

Houses in multiple occupation
Properties defined as Houses in Multiple Occupation (HMOs) are subject to the **Regulatory Reform (Fire Safety) Order 2005** in that the common areas that may be visited by the landlord or others are subject to a suitable and sufficient fire risk assessment. The individual residential areas are not subject to this requirement. HMOs are still subject to the fire safety requirements imposed by the **Housing Act 2004**.

Who is the 'responsible person'?

In each hotel or guest house there should be one person who is, to some extent, in control of the workplace. They should be nominated to take responsibility for carrying out the fire risk assessments and ensuring that fire protection and prevention measures are observed and maintained.

Although not a legal requirement, it is advisable to identify the nominated responsible person on the assessment document and make that person known to all staff.

What is a fire risk assessment?

A fire risk assessment is a structured consideration of the fire hazards and management of fire in the premises. It can be undertaken in five steps:
- identify the fire hazards
- identify the people at risk
- evaluate, remove, reduce and protect from risk
- record, plan, inform, instruct and train
- review the assessment periodically.

Remember: you know your premises best, so follow the guidance and assess how your staff and guests would escape from the building quickly if a fire started – 2.5 minutes is the target time. Think about how they would be alerted and how easily they would find their way out. After all, guest safety is the most important thing to consider – and yours too, if you live on the premises.

Identify the fire hazards

Fire hazards include:

- potential sources of ignition, e.g.:
  - cooking equipment
  - lighting
  - electrical apparatus
  - display screen equipment, e.g. computer screens
- combustible materials that may burn, e.g.:
  - the furnishings and furniture
  - parts of the building such as panelling
  - combustible linings on escape routes
  - display materials
- flammable liquids and gases, e.g. those used for cleaning or maintenance purposes.

Identify the people at risk

The people at risk include:

- guests
- staff
- contractors
- other visitors
- people outside the property, e.g. neighbours and passers-by.

Particular note should be made of the number of people on the premises and any persons – staff or guests – who have any form of disability. Guests with a disability should be accommodated in rooms on low floors where possible to minimise their travel distance to a place of safety.

Evaluate, remove, reduce and protect from risk

This step involves evaluating the hazards and taking measures to eliminate these where possible. For example, the prohibition of smoking in guests' rooms or replacing candles on dinner tables with an alternative without an open flame, will help to reduce the hazards.

Particular care should be taken when selecting curtains and display materials, especially decorations at times of public holidays and festivals.

Any simple changes should be made straight away, such as clearing obstacles and removing flammable items from escape routes. If you identify something that would be too expensive or cause too much disruption to rectify straight away, make a note of the work and when you intend to carry it out. Out of season is always a good time to catch up on such work.

Record, plan, inform and train

Where there are five or more staff, the fire risk assessment should be recorded. In other cases, (e.g. small guest houses, B&Bs and self-catering accommodation) it is good practice to record the assessment anyway to demonstrate compliance with the law. The logbook should contain details of maintenance and servicing to fire protection measures. It should also include details about alarms, detectors and fire extinguishers.

An emergency plan should be drawn up to indicate the actions that should be taken by staff as well as guests and others in case of a fire on the premises. **The plan, in the form of a Fire Action Notice, should be displayed in guest rooms and adjacent to the fire alarm call points in the staff and common areas**.

These actions should include the measures that would be taken to identify and assist anyone with a disability to leave the premises safely.

Staff should be trained in the actions that they would be expected to take in an emergency and this should include all staff participating in periodic fire drills at least once, and preferably twice a year. Where staff do not speak fluent English, special attention should be given to ensuring that instructions are fully understood by the staff concerned.

Where a hotel is part of a complex of buildings (such as a shopping centre) or parts of the buildings are occupied by franchise holders, then the responsible person should liaise with the appropriate staff in these areas.

Review the assessment periodically

The fire risk assessment for the premises should be reviewed periodically and when:

- alterations are made to the structure or layout of the premises
- there are changes in the use of an area of the building
- there are significant changes to the number or location of the visitors or staff
- there is a significant change in the mobility level or other factors influencing the response of visitors or staff in an emergency
- there are changes in the management of the building.

There are no prescribed times for the reviews, but many businesses choose to review their assessment annually.

How do I know what fire precautions I need?

The fire precautions needed used to be specified in the fire certificate. With the demise of this document it is now up to the responsible person to determine the appropriate fire precautions as a result of their fire risk assessment.

The guidance publication, *Do You Have Paying Guests?* Is available on the **Inside Government** website **www.gov.uk/government/publications/do-you-have-paying-guests** and provides advice tailored specifically for B&Bs, guest houses and self catering properties. It is designed to encourage compliance, by giving the owners of these businesses practical advice on reducing fire risks in their establishments. It explains the risk assessment process, sets out sources of further advice and guidance and offers some practical information for owners on what may represent appropriate and proportionate fire safety measures in these types of premises.

The most important factor is fire prevention: staff should be made aware of fire hazards and safe working practices in order to prevent a fire breaking out. There should be an emergency plan drawn up so that all staff know what actions they should take in the event of a fire.

The fire protection provisions will vary according to the particular premises but should include the following:

- **means of escape:** in all premises it is important that there are adequate means of escape. In all but the smallest guest houses there should normally be at least two escape routes from all parts of the building and these should be available for use and free of obstructions at all times.
- **fire alarm:** there should be a means of alerting people to a fire, should it break out. See below for more details.
- **emergency lighting:** in order for everyone to find their way out of the building safely there should be automatic emergency escape lighting. In some very small guest houses there may be sufficient 'borrowed light' from street lights outside but this is not often the case.
- **signs:** these should be prominently displayed to guide guests to the fire exits with which they will not be familiar.
- **fire fighting equipment:** a suitable number of appropriate fire extinguishers should be provided and at least some staff should be instructed in their use.

Which alarm system?

Since the interpretation of the Order may vary with each fire service around the country, it is difficult to advise businesses in a general way on exactly what type of alarm system they should fit.

The types of system required will, however, depend on the level of the risk – a very sophisticated system would not be necessary in small premises. Whatever system is used should take into account anyone with a disability (e.g. hearing loss), so that their safety is not compromised.

The **Regulatory Reform (Fire Safety) Order 2005** requires that premises are provided with suitable and sufficient means of detecting fire and giving warning in the event of a fire. For small buildings this may be interconnected mains-powered smoke and heat alarms that all sound in the event of fire.

Guidelines for small premises are that they can install simple systems – LD2 or LD3 – that comprise mains-operated smoke and heat alarms with battery back-up. Current legislation defines a 'small' property as being up to two storeys high (from the ground) with no floor more than 200 square metres in total. This equates to a floor with eight to ten en-suite double rooms.

LD2 properties must have alarms in corridors and all rooms leading off the main escape route, while LD3 properties require them only in the corridor, landing and hallway of the main escape route. These LD3 alarms are the same as those required in all new homes. If the property was built after 1990, it is likely to already comply.

Larger properties may be expected to install more sophisticated detectors and alarms, which are classed as L2 systems.

How do I do the assessment?

Guidance is set out in a Government publication: *Do You have Paying Guests?* (see above) which includes a template for undertaking an assessment of your property.

VisitEngland also provides a free-to-use Fire Risk Assessment Tool, designed to give step-by-step guidance to help tourism businesses identify risks, form an action plan and produce a written record: **www.visitengland.com/pinkbookonline**.

Further advice can be gained from a fire safety consultant or your local fire authority.

How do I record the fire risk assessment?

The legislation does not prescribe a specific format for the assessment but you do have to record the **significant findings** and the **persons especially at risk** from fire. The significant findings are a list of the actions that should be taken to reduce the fire hazards to a minimum.

You should also record any shortcomings that are identified in the management of the general fire precautions. A note should be kept of the remedial actions that are taken to demonstrate to the fire brigade, should they visit, that you are taking steps to address these matters.

Is the assessment a one-off exercise?

No: you are required to keep your assessment under review and update it when necessary. A new assessment should always be undertaken whenever a property is renovated or structurally altered.

Who enforces the legislation?

The **Regulatory Reform (Fire Safety) Order 2005** is enforced by the local fire and rescue service. Fire Safety Officers will make periodic visits to the premises and will ask to see the fire risk assessment to ensure that it is 'suitable and sufficient'.

What may fire officers look at?

As well as inspecting the means of escape and other fire precautions, the Fire Safety Officer may ask to see the **fire log book** containing the records of the servicing and maintenance of the fire protection measures (e.g. the automatic fire detection and alarm system and the emergency lighting).

The officer may also ask to see the **record of false fire alarms** in the premises so these should also be kept up to date.

Notices

If your premises do not meet the Order, the Fire Safety Officer will provide practical advice or, if the risk is serious or if the Officer is not satisfied, you may be issued with one of the following:

- **an alterations notice:** this does not require alterations to be made to the premises. It is served when the enforcing authority believes that there will be a serious risk to people in the building if a change is made to any particular part of the premises or their use.
- **an enforcement notice:** this requires certain measures to be taken within a specified timeframe.
- **a prohibition notice:** this requires the business to cease trading immediately until certain remedial action has been taken.

In all cases you will have a right of appeal, both informally and formally. An informal appeal can sometimes identify a different way of meeting the Order which satisfies both parties.

The fire authority will work with you to achieve a satisfactory level of fire safety.

Further Guidance

The Inside Government portal **www.gov.uk/government/ organisations/department-for-communities-and-local-government/series/fire-safety-law-and-guidance-documents-for-business** contains a range of guidance publications on fire safety that can be downloaded free of charge including:

- *Do You Have Paying Guests?* – a guide specifically designed to provide advice on fire safety to small accommodation businesses.
- *Regulatory Reform (Fire Safety) Order 2005 – A short guide to making your premises safe from fire*
- *Fire Safety Risk Assessment – Sleeping Accommodation*
- *Fire Safety Risk Assessment – Means of Escape for Disabled People*.

Fire Safety of Furniture and Furnishings

KEY FACTS

- If you provide self-catering accommodation that contains upholstered furniture the legislation applies to you.
- All furniture (new and second-hand) in your self-catering accommodation that is covered by the regulations must comply with certain safety tests.
- An agency's liability for the fire safety of the furniture in the properties it handles depends on the terms of its arrangement with the accommodation owner.

Do the Regulations apply to me?

Yes: if you are providing self-catering accommodation that contains upholstered furniture.

What do the Regulations cover?

The **Furniture and Furnishings (Fire) (Safety) Regulations 1988** (as amended) set fire resistance standards for upholstered furniture in domestic use (new and second-hand).

The Regulations apply only to upholstered furniture supplied for domestic use, a type of use that implies a low fire hazard. Most holiday lets are regarded as constituting domestic use and, therefore, are covered by the Regulations.

Furniture designed to cope with a greater fire hazard (e.g. hotel beds and chairs) is available and may be offered to you by some retailers. When re-equipping your self-catering property, it will normally be for you to decide whether or not you require the new furniture to meet these higher fire resistance standards. If in any doubt, check with your local fire authority.

For simplicity's sake in the information that follows, furniture and furnishings is referred to as 'furniture'.

What furniture is affected?

To come within the scope of the regulations, furniture must be upholstered. Such furniture would include:

- domestic furniture, including children's furniture
- beds and divans (including their bases and headboards), mattresses of any size
- sofa beds, futons and other convertibles
- nursery furniture (e.g. highchairs, cots and playpens)
- domestic garden furniture
- scatter cushions and seat pads
- pillows
- furniture in new caravans.

The Regulations also apply to loose and stretch covers for furniture.

What furniture is not affected?

The Regulations do not apply to:

- bed clothes (including duvets)
- loose covers for mattresses
- pillowcases
- curtains
- carpets
- sleeping bags
- goods made before 1 January 1950 and the materials used to re-upholster them.

Main provisions of the Regulations

All furniture (new and second-hand) in self-catering accommodations that are covered by the Regulations must comply with certain safety tests. These are very broadly as follows:

- upholstered furniture must pass a prescribed cigarette resistance test
- cover fabric, whether for use in permanent or loose covers, will normally have to pass a match resistance test
- filling materials for all furniture must pass ignitability tests as specified in the regulations
- all new upholstered furniture (except mattresses and bedding) and loose and stretch covers for furniture must carry a permanent label detailing compliance with fire safety requirements. Always look for these labels before buying any upholstered furniture for your property.

If you are having items re-upholstered, make sure that the materials used comply with the regulations. Remember, however, that the Regulations do not apply to materials used to re-upholster furniture made before 1950, unless that furniture is being significantly reworked and upholstered.

Can I use fire-inhibiting sprays to increase the life of my existing furniture?

These sprays are available from a number of companies who will treat the furniture for you. However, the Local Government Association and the Department for Business Innovation and Skills (BIS) advise owners to exercise extreme caution in using them because of issues relating to their durability. The treatment may, for example, be rendered ineffective by laundering.

Before deciding to have your furniture treated, you should:

- remember that the regulations apply both to covers and to filling materials
- make absolutely sure that the spray on offer is appropriate for the covers and filling materials used in your furniture
- be sure that the spray will not be affected by previous treatments (e.g. waterproofing) carried out on the furniture
- bear in mind that some sprays are not water resistant and will wash out, even when fluids, such as tea, are spilled on the treated fabric
- ask the company to provide strong evidence and guarantees that the spray does do what it is supposed to do.

If the furniture which you have had treated is subsequently found not to meet the fire resistance standards specified in the Regulations, it will be you (as the supplier of the furniture), and not the supplier or manufacturer of the spray, who is held responsible under this legislation.

Are letting agencies caught by the Regulations?

- **Possibly:** Whether or not an agency is liable for the fire safety of the furniture in the properties it handles will depend on the terms of its arrangement with you, the owner of the accommodation.

It seems that agencies that do no more than market your property and take bookings are unlikely to be liable. However, agencies that also manage and maintain properties on an owner's behalf could possibly be liable.

As this is something of a grey area, some marketing/booking agencies cover themselves by including a clause in their contracts with owners which commits those owners to ensuring that their property complies at all times with these regulations (and others).

Expect any prospective agency to ask about the fire resistance standards of your furniture before it agrees to take your property on to its books.

Review of the Regulations

The Department for Business, Innovation and Skills is currently undertaking a review of the Furniture and Furnishings (Fire) (Safety) Regulations. However, this review is likely only to affect materials that can be used in the manufacture of furniture and furnishings, and safety tests conducted on them, rather than affecting the responsibilities of accommodation providers.

Further guidance

- A copy of the publication , *A Guide to the Furniture and Furnishings (Fire) (Safety) Regulations*, can be downloaded from **www.berr.gov.uk/files/file24685.pdf**.
- For further assistance, contact the local trading standards department of your local authority.

Smoking in Public Places

KEY FACTS

- Smoking is banned in enclosed public spaces and places of work, with some exemptions.
- There is a legal duty for you to display a legible no-smoking sign where it can be seen by customers and staff.
- There is a legal duty on any person who owns or manages smoke-free premises to ensure that guests, visitors and staff do not smoke on the premises.

Smoking ban

There has been a ban on smoking in enclosed public spaces and places of work (with some exemptions) since 1 July 2007, when the **Health Act 2006** came into force.

Does the Act apply to me?

Yes: if you own or manage enclosed or substantially enclosed premises that are open to the public, or are used as a place of work by more than one person, or where members of the public might visit to receive or provide goods or services.

Note: while the areas of premises to which the ban applies and the definitions and the exemptions in them are the same in Wales, the signage requirement is different.

Definitions

Enclosed places: premises are considered to be enclosed if they have a ceiling or roof and, except for doors, windows or passageways, are wholly enclosed, whether on a permanent or temporary basis.

Substantially enclosed areas – the 50% rule: Substantially enclosed premises are defined as those that have a ceiling or roof (including retractable roofs such as awnings), but have permanent openings in the walls, not including doors or windows, that are less than half of the total area of the walls. Walls include fixed or retractable structures that serve the purpose of walls and constitute the perimeter of premises (e.g. windbreaks). Temporary structures such as tents, marquees or similar will be classified as enclosed premises if they fall within the definition.

Exemptions

While smoking is banned from all the public and communal areas of hotels and guest houses, there are a number of exemptions.

- **Self-contained short-term rental accommodation** (holiday cottages/flats/caravans) are not required to be smoke-free but you retain the right to determine whether to allow smoking in the property.
- The **private areas of bed and breakfasts and guest houses** are not covered by the ban, provided that the areas are not used by any staff (i.e. the laundry may be out of bounds for customers but if a cleaner has to use it, it is covered by the ban).
- **Designated bedrooms** in hotels, guest houses and bed and breakfasts. To qualify, a designated bedroom must:
  - be designated in writing by the person in charge of the premises as being a smoking room
  - be completely enclosed except for doors and windows
  - have a ventilation system that must not discharge into any non-smoking part of the premises
  - have doors to smoke-free parts of the premises that shut mechanically after use
  - be clearly marked as a room in which smoking is permitted.

It should be noted there is no legal requirement for you to provide designated smoking bedrooms. Providing such rooms is purely at your discretion.

Signage

The Smoke-free (Signs) Regulations 2012 (England only) require you to display at least one legible no-smoking sign. There is no requirement on the location or size of the sign, provided that is able to be seen by customers and staff.

Enforcement and penalties

Enforcement is the responsibility of local authorities – environmental health officers have the power to enter all 'no-smoking premises' in order to establish that the smoke-free legislation is being enforced in accordance with the law.

UPDATED

Failure to display appropriate non-smoking signage may result in a fine, and the legislation also places a legal duty on any person who owns or manages smoke-free premises to ensure that guests, visitors and staff do not smoke on the premises.

Owners or managers who are found not to have taken reasonable steps to stop people smoking on their premises will be liable to a fine of up to £2,500 on conviction.

Further guidance

- Further information on the Smoking Ban is available on the Health and Safety Executive website **www.hse.gov.uk/contact/faqs/smoking.htm**.

STAFF

Working Hours

KEY FACTS

- The **Working Time Regulations 1998** (as amended) apply to all accommodation providers that have people working for them.
- You must take reasonable steps to ensure that workers do not work more than an average of 48 hours a week (excluding lunch breaks).
- Workers are entitled to 5.6 weeks' paid leave a year and rest periods of a specified length in each working day and in each seven day period.
- You need to keep sufficient records to show that you are complying with the regulations.

Working Time Regulations

Are the Regulations relevant to me?
The **Working Time Regulations 1998** (as amended) apply to all accommodation providers that have people working for them, however small the business.

What staff are covered by the Regulations?
Anyone who is working for you including trainees and those under 18 (young workers), but excluding the genuinely self-employed.

What are the requirements?
Working time
You are responsible for taking reasonable steps to ensure that workers do not work more than an average of 48 hours a week, excluding lunch breaks. (The number of hours worked each week should be averaged out over 17 weeks).

- Employees can choose to work longer, but the agreement must be in writing and signed by the worker. This is known as a Working Time Regulations Opt-Out Agreement.
- Young employees may not ordinarily work more than eight hours a day or **40 hours a week**. There is no opt-out possible from the young workers' limitations.

Night-time workers

You are also responsible for taking reasonable steps to ensure that any night workers do not work, on average, more than eight hours in 24. There is no opt-out from the night work limits. Night workers are those who normally work at least three hours between 23:00 and 06:00.

- You must offer free health assessments to a night worker before they start working nights and on a regular basis to ensure they are fit for night work.
- Young workers may not ordinarily work between 22:00 and 06:00 or between 23:00 and 07:00. However, they may work between 22:00 and 23:00 to midnight and between 04:00 to 06:00 or 07:00 in certain special circumstances (e.g. working in a hotel, restaurant or bar).

Paid annual leave

As of 1 April 2009, workers, whether full-time or part-time, are entitled to 5.6 weeks' paid leave a year, starting on the first day of employment. A 'week's leave' is the equivalent of the time normally worked in a week. This should be applied pro-rata for part-time employees. For example, if a worker normally works five days a week, this equals 28 working days a year as paid leave, and for a Saturday worker this equates to 5.6 days a year.

You must set out an employee's paid holiday entitlement in their 'written statement of employment'. This should enable them to work out their entitlement and pay for any untaken holiday if they leave.

Note: The holiday entitlement can include bank holidays provided that you pay them for those days.

Rolled-up Holiday Pay

Rolled-up Holiday Pay is where businesses pay employees an additional amount on top of their normal wages over the course of the year as holiday pay instead of paying it as a lump sum when the holiday is taken. ACAS advice is that this practice is **not** legal.

Further information, including a template for a 'written statement of employment' is available on the ACAS website **www.ACAS.gov.uk**.

Rest periods

Workers are entitled to 11 hours' consecutive rest in between each working day, and at least 24 hours' uninterrupted rest for every seven day period (this may be averaged over two weeks).

STAFF

Young workers are entitled to 12 hours' rest for each working day and two days' rest for every seven day period.

In-work rest
Workers are entitled to 20 minutes rest daily if they work more than six hours (young workers are entitled to 30 minutes if they work more than 4.5 hours).

Special circumstances
For night workers' rest periods and in-work rest breaks, there are exceptions to the regulations, e.g. during busy peak periods, but workers must normally be given equivalent rest periods in compensation.

Records
You need to keep sufficient records in each case to show that you are complying with the Regulations.

Further guidance

Guidance on all aspects of the Working Time Regulations is available on the ACAS website **www.acas.gov.uk**.
- If you require further information about the application of the regulations and help with matters about time off, rest breaks, paid annual leave and other general employment information, call the ACAS national helpline on 08457 474 747
- If you need information about making a claim or going to a tribunal, call the Employment Tribunals enquiry line on 08457 959 775 or refer to the Tribunals section of the Department for Justice website **www.justice.gov.uk**
- Guidance on matters to do with weekly and night working time limits and health assessments is available from the Health and Safety Executive website **www.hse.gov.uk**.

National Minimum Wage

KEY FACTS

There are four rates of national minimum wage
(as of 1 October 2014):

- the main adult rate (for workers aged 21 and over)
  is £6.50 per hour
- the development rate for 18-20 year old workers
  is £5.13 per hour
- the development rate for workers under 18
  is £3.79 per hour
- the rate for Apprentices is £2.73 per hour.

Is this relevant to me?

The national minimum wage came into effect on 1 April 1999. It is
relevant to all accommodation providers that have employees,
regardless of the size of the business. The national minimum wage is
enforceable by HM Revenue and Customs (HMRC).

If HMRC find that you have underpaid any of your staff, they can issue
a Notice of Underpayment requiring the employer to repay arrears to
their staff (paid at the current minimum wage rate) and pay a penalty
to the Government. The penalty will be set at 50% of the total
underpayment with a minimum of £100 and a maximum of £5,000.

Who is entitled to the National Minimum Wage?

Anyone working for you (including part-time and casual staff)
is entitled to receive the minimum wage except:

- anyone 'genuinely self-employed' (e.g. someone who
  controls his own time, what work he does, and invoices you
  rather than receiving wages)
- voluntary workers
- workers who are based permanently outside the UK or who
  are based in the Channel Islands or the Isle of Man.

What is the National Minimum Wage?

There are three rates of national minimum wage.
Rates as of 1 October 2013 are:

- **£6.50 per hour** for employees aged 21 and over
- **£5.13 per hour** for employees aged 18-20
- **£3.79 per hour** for employees aged under 18
- **£2.73 per hour** for Apprentices aged under 19 or those in the first year of their apprenticeship.

Further information on the national minimum wage, including current rates, can be found at **www.gov.uk/national-minimum-wage-rates**.

What counts as part of a wage?
- **Included:** In addition to basic pay, certain other payments may count towards the national minimum wage, including:
  - bonuses
  - incentives
  - accommodation
  - money for items such as clothing and shoes where the worker can decide where to buy the items.
- **Excluded:** Other additional payments are excluded, including:
  - premium payments for overtime or shift work
  - special allowances
  - expenses
  - tips, service charges or any other type of gratuity (see *Tips and service charges* below)
  - expenditure on items such as clothing and tools related to work
  - all benefits in kind, including meals, except accommodation.

Accommodation offset
If you provide accommodation to a member of staff, you are entitled to offset an amount for this against the national minimum wage. The daily rate of the accommodation offset is £4.91 a day (£34.37 a week) for each day that accommodation is provided.

Does the National Minimum Wage apply to rest breaks, sick time and holidays?

Whether or not you have to pay the national minimum wage for hours taken as rest breaks, sick time, holidays, etc will depend on the type of work the worker is doing. The two most applicable types of work are:

- **time work:** when you pay the worker according to the number of hours he/she works

UPDATED

UPDATED

- **salaried hours work:** when the workers have a contract to work a set number of hours each year in return for an annual salary paid in instalments.

If employees are on 'time work', then you are not required to pay them for rest breaks, sick time or holidays. However, if they are on 'salaried hours work', then you must pay them during these periods.

For advice call the Pay and Work Rights Helpline on 0800 917 2368 or consult the Employment section of the Government Direct website **www.direct.gov.uk**.

Tips and service charges

Legislation has been introduced that prevents businesses using tips and service charges to constitute part of the national minimum wage. This means that employees must receive at least the national minimum wage as base pay, with any income from tips or service charges being additional. This is regardless of whether the gratuity is paid directly by the customer to the employee (e.g. a cash tip left on the table in a restaurant) or through the payroll (e.g. a discretionary service charge added to the customer's bill).

The Department for Business, Innovation and Skills (BIS) has produced a code of practice for the treatment of tips and service charges by businesses *A Code of Best Practice on Service Charges, Tips, Gratuities and Cover Charges* (**www.bis.gov.uk/files/file 52948.pdf**). This code has been endorsed by the British Hospitality Association, the Trade Union Congress and the Confederation of British Industry (CBI) and is based on four principles:

1 That businesses clearly display their policy on tips and service charges for customers.
2 That businesses have a process in place for explaining to customers how charges are distributed and what, if any, deductions are made.
3 That businesses should ensure that staff understand the policy and are able to explain it to customers.
4 That staff are fully informed of the distribution of tips and service charges and any deductions and are consulted on any changes.

How should cash tips be dealt with?

Cash tips are payments given directly by customers to individual employees, not to the business. Any arrangement for sharing cash tips among employees should be in accordance with their wishes. The business owner will not be involved in this process. It is the responsibility of the employees receiving such cash tips to make proper disclosure to HM Revenue and Customs and to account for Income Tax in respect of these earnings.

How should service charges be dealt with?

For gratuities, such as service charges, that are incorporated into the billing system, the business can deduct costs incurred in handling and distributing these payments to employees. Such deductions would cover credit card and banking charges, payroll processing costs, and the average costs of credit card fraud.

Businesses are also able to make deductions associated with other costs including breakages, till shortages and customers leaving without paying. While the level of these costs will vary depending on the nature of the business, BIS guidance suggests that total deductions should **not** be more than 30% of gratuities received.

These deductions should be revealed to customers as part of the disclosure process.

Where discretionary service charges and non-cash tips are paid to employees by the business, they should be paid from the company bank account, with Income Tax deducted under PAYE. The broad process for distribution of these amounts should be revealed to customers as part of the disclosure process (see below).

What disclosure should be made?

Businesses should disclose to customers how they deal with service charges and non-cash tips, at least by a written note available for inspection at each restaurant and on the company website, if there is one. The disclosure should cover:

- whether an amount is deducted for handling costs (and how much)
- how the remainder is shared between the business and the employees
- the broad process for distribution, e.g. that they are shared between the employees in the business through a system controlled by a representative of the employees.

Records

- You are required to keep sufficient records to prove you are paying the national minimum wage.
- You must allow workers to see their record within 14 days if they make a request in writing.

Further guidance

- The Pay and Work Rights Helpline on 0800 917 2368 gives free confidential advice on national minimum wage issues
- Guidance on all aspects of the national minimum wage is available on the Minimum Wage section of the Gov.uk website **www.gov.uk/browse/working/tax-minimum-wage**
- The *Code of Best Practice on Service Charges, Tips, Gratuities and Cover Charges* is available from the BIS at **www.bis.gov.uk/files/file52948.pdf**.

Discrimination

KEY FACTS

- Discrimination laws apply to all service providers.
- It is unlawful to discriminate directly against anyone.
- It is unlawful to discriminate indirectly against anyone.

The Equality Act 2010

The Equality Act 2010 consolidated nine pieces of existing anti-discrimination legislation into one single Act. In doing so, it also simplified and strengthened the existing legislation law in order to reduce discrimination and inequality.

Under the Act, it is unlawful to discriminate against any employee or customer (that is to treat them less favourably) on the grounds of:
- disability
- gender reassignment
- pregnancy and maternity
- race – this includes ethnic or national origins, colour and nationality
- religion or belief
- sex
- sexual orientation
- age – this applies to those aged 18 or above.

This protection also applies where a person is unfairly treated because they are wrongly perceived to have a particular characteristic (or are treated as though they do), or because they associate with someone who has the characteristic. For example, the protection extends to the carer, partner or family of a person discriminated against.

As it applies to employees
You are required to treat all employees or job applicants the same. This covers all areas of employment, including recruitment, terms and conditions, promotion and transfers, training and development, and the dismissal process. This requirement applies to all employers, regardless of size.

There are rules against employers asking job applicants disability-related questions and you are required to make reasonable adjustments to help disabled people fulfil the job they are employed to undertake or are applying for. For example, you would not be allowed to reject an applicant for a receptionist position from someone in a wheelchair on the grounds that the reception desk was too high. Rather, you are required to make modifications to the desk to enable them to undertake this role.

The legislation also clarifies and strengthens the protection afforded to women undertaking breastfeeding, which makes it illegal to ask a woman to stop breastfeeding in a public space.

Harassment

You are required to protect your staff from harassment at all times. This means taking steps to protect staff from harassment by other staff members and also from harassment from suppliers and customers. Further, an employee may claim harassment even if they are not the person that is being harassed. This can happen, for example:

- where witnessing the harassment of an employee results in the creation of an intimidating environment for another employee
- where an employer has been informed that an employee has been harassed on two or more occasions by a third party, such as a customer or supplier, and does nothing to prevent further harassment
- where unwanted conduct relates to the sex of a person, even if it is not prompted by the complainant's sex.

Employers face unlimited fines under the legislation if they are found not to be protecting staff from harassment or treating them in a discriminatory manner. For more details and guidance on discrimination legislation, go to **www.gov.uk/equality-act-2010-guidance**.

As it applies to customers

As with employment, it is illegal to discriminate on the basis of disability, sex, gender reassignment, race, sexual orientation, religion, pregnancy or age in the provision of goods and services to customers unless there is objective justification for doing so. This means that there have to be valid, justifiable reasons why a service cannot be provided to certain groups. For example, there may be medical reasons for not providing certain goods or services.

The Equality Act 2010 makes it easier for customers to require you to make reasonable adjustments in the way that you provide goods or

UPDATED

UPDATED

UPDATED

LICENCES & CONSENTS

MARKETING

GUESTS

FOOD & DRINK

HEALTH & SAFETY

STAFF

BUSINESS MANAGEMENT & TAX

FURTHER INFORMATION

STAFF

service. For example, making a buffet more easily accessible or providing menus in large print. The test will be whether the way that you provide goods or services places a disabled person at a substantial disadvantage to other customers.

However, the Act does enable businesses to undertake positive action to target their goods, facilities or services to a particular group that is either disadvantaged or currently under-represented in their consumer base, or that has particular needs. For example, discounts could be given to disabled customers or their carers.

Age Discrimination
On 1 October 2012, the Government introduced age discrimination. This makes it illegal to provide a different product or service, charge a different price, or to apply different terms and condition to any customer over 18 years old on the basis of age unless:

- there is an Objective Justification. Objective Justification means that there is a valid objective reason for doing so (for example, charging different premiums for travel insurance could be justified on the basis of different levels of risk)
- the discrimination is beneficial: this means that offering discounts to people that allow them improved access to goods and services would be acceptable (for example, discounts to retired people would be acceptable, as it would increase social inclusion).

Further guidance

- Further information on discrimination and the provisions of the Equality Act 2010 are available on the Equality and Human Rights Commission website **www.equalityhumanrights.com/ advice-and-guidance/guidance-for-employers/index.html**.

Time Off for Parents

KEY FACTS

- All employers are required to comply with legislation related to family-friendly working.
- Employees' rights in this area include maternity and paternity rights, adoption leave, flexible working and parental leave.

Family-friendly working

There are laws that support working parents in combining work with looking after their children. As well as your legal duty to uphold these rights, it is also good practice to support family-friendly working and flexible working arrangements for all types of employees.

Maternity rights

Maternity leave

Regardless of how long they have worked for you, all pregnant employees, (i.e. those working under a contract of employment) are entitled to take up to 52 weeks' Statutory Maternity Leave (SML). This comprises of:

- **26 weeks Ordinary Maternity Leave**
- **26 weeks Additional Maternity Leave**

Additional Maternity Leave starts immediately after Ordinary Maternity Leave.

Statutory Maternity Pay

To qualify for Statutory Maternity Pay (SMP) an employee must have been:

- employed continuously (some breaks do not interrupt continuous employment) for at least 26 weeks into the 15th week before the due date
- earning an average of at least £109 a week (before tax).

Statutory Maternity Pay is paid for up to 39 weeks with employees receiving:

UPDATED

- 90% of their average weekly earnings (before tax) for the first 6 weeks
- £138.18 or 90% of their average weekly earnings (whichever is lower) for the next 33 weeks.

SMP is to be paid in the same way as the employee receives their normal wages (e.g. monthly or weekly).

Employees can choose when SMP will start, although this will normally coincide with their taking Ordinary Maternity Leave. The earliest SMP can start is 11 weeks before the due date. Employees entitled to SMP are entitled to receive it even if they decide to leave before they start receiving SMP. They do not have to repay it if they decide not to go back to work or leave their job while getting SMP.

Paternity rights

Paternity Leave

Employees who have 26 weeks service by the 15th week before the Expected Week of Childbirth are entitled to two weeks' paternity leave at or around the date the child is born. Employees may also take paternity leave if:

- they are not the biological father, but are the biological mother's partner
- they expect to have responsibility for the child's upbringing
- they have adopted the child or are the partner of the person who has adopted.

Ordinary Paternity leave is for a period of 1 or 2 weeks. Additional Paternity Leave is available for a maximum of 26 weeks and can be taken any time from 20 weeks after the child is born until its first birthday, provided that the child's mother has returned to work. In the case of adoption, it can start anytime between 20 weeks and 52 weeks after the child starts living with the adopter.

To qualify for Additional Paternity Leave, employees must provide notice in writing at least eight weeks before the start of the leave. This must include:

- the expected date of the baby's birth or date of notification of being matched for adoption
- the actual date of the baby's birth, or placement of adoption
- the start date of the Additional Paternity Leave and pay.

Statutory paternity pay

Similarly to maternity pay, the statutory weekly rate of Ordinary Paternity Pay and Additional Paternity Pay is £138.18, or 90% of average weekly earnings (whichever is lower).

Note: Maternity and Paternity Leave and Pay requirements also apply to same-sex couples.

Adoption leave

Employees who are newly matched with a child for adoption and who have 26 weeks' service when this happens are entitled to up to **26 weeks'** Ordinary Adoption Leave, and up to a further **26 weeks'** additional adoption leave.

Employees who adopt individually are entitled to adoption leave and pay and where a couple adopt together, one member of the couple is entitled to adoption leave and pay. The couple can decide which partner will take adoption leave.

Employees don't qualify for Statutory Adoption Leave or Pay if they:
- arrange a private adoption
- become a special guardian or kinship carer
- adopt a stepchild
- have a child through surrogacy
- adopt a family member or stepchild.

Statutory Adoption Pay

The weekly amount of Statutory Adoption Pay is £138.18 or 90% of average weekly earnings before tax (whichever is lower) and is payable for 39 weeks.

Reclaiming Statutory Maternity, Paternity and Adoption Pay

You can usually reclaim 92% of employees' Statutory Maternity (SMP), Paternity and Adoption Pay. You can reclaim 103% if your business qualifies for Small Employers' Relief. You get this if you paid less than £45,000 in Class 1 National Insurance in the last complete tax year before the qualifying or matching week.

Flexible working

Introducing flexible working practices can benefit everyone in your business. Many employers believe flexible working makes good business sense and brings about a range of improvements, including greater cost-efficiencies and better staff morale.

There are many different forms of flexible working. Flexible working can include:

- part-time working
- flexi-time
- job-sharing
- working from home
- term-time working
- staggered hours.

Up until 2014, only the following employees had the right to apply to work flexibly:

- those that have a child aged 16 and under (disabled child aged under 18)
- those that are the carer for an adult as defined by the Department for Business, Innovation and Skills (BIS)
- those that have worked for their employer for 26 weeks continuously at the date that the application is made
- those that have not have made another application to work flexibly under the right during the past 12 months.

However, the Government has now extended the statutory right to make a flexible working request to all employees with 26 weeks' continuous employment. As an employer, you have a duty to consider these requests seriously.

Information on making and assessing an application for flexible working is available from the ACAS website **www.acas.org.uk/ index.aspx?articleid=1616**.

Parental leave

Parental leave is a right for the parents to take time off work to look after a child or make arrangements for the child's welfare.

Which staff can claim it?

Employees who have, or expect to have, parental responsibility for a child and have been employed for at least a year. However, special rules apply for parents of children born, or placed for adoption, before 14 December 1999.

What are the main provisions?

- Each parent is entitled to **18 weeks' unpaid parental leave** for each child, which can be taken up until the child's fifth birthday (or, the end of the fifth year after adoption, or the child's 18th birthday if that is sooner).
- At the end of parental leave the employee is **entitled to return to the same job**, if the leave was for four weeks

or less. If it was for longer, the employee is entitled to return to the same job, or if that is not reasonably practicable, a similar job.

- You can reach your **own agreement** with an employee about the practicalities. If you do not, there are fall back provisions (21 days' notice; minimum of one week blocks; maximum of four weeks a year for each child; the employer can postpone the leave for up to six months when particularly disruptive on the business, except for leave requested immediately after the child is born/adopted).
- You do not have to keep **records**, but you can be asked by a subsequent employer about how much leave an employee has taken (you can also ask a previous employer).
- You are entitled to ask to see **evidence** to confirm that an employee is the parent or the person legally responsible for the child.
- There are additional entitlements for parents of **disabled children**.

Note: employees also have the right to take a reasonable period off work to deal with an emergency involving a dependent.

Further guidance

- The *Rights and Responsibilities at Work* section of ACAS's website has a very useful range of online guides to maternity, paternity, adoption and flexible working policies including the advice booklet *The right to apply for flexible working* **www.acas.org.uk**
- For further information, you can call the ACAS helpline: 08457 474 747.

Migrant Workers

LICENCES & CONSENTS

MARKETING

GUESTS

FOOD & DRINK

HEALTH & SAFETY

STAFF

BUSINESS MANAGEMENT & TAX

FURTHER INFORMATION

KEY FACTS

- If you employ, or plan to employ, people from outside the UK, you need to make sure that they have permission to work here before they start working for you.

- To be entitled to work in the UK, a foreign national must provide you with the necessary documentation.

- You should check any documentation provided to ensure, to the best of your ability, that those documents are genuine and that the potential employee is entitled to work in the UK.

- Employees from certain specified countries also need to register with the Home Office's Worker Registration Scheme.

- Migrants from outside the European Union need to pass a points-based assessment before they are given permission to enter or remain in the United Kingdom. There are several tiers and, with the exception of highly skilled Tier 1 workers, other non-EU workers and students need a UK sponsor to vouch for them.

Employers' responsibilities

It is important that you are aware of your responsibilities when employing foreign staff. The legislation that applies to migrant workers is the **UK Borders Act 2007**. The Act covers all aspects of immigration, from asylum seekers through to permanent migration, including the right to work and study in the UK.

On the basis of this legislation the Home Office develops and implements the UK's immigration rules, which provide the detail as to how the Act is implemented. The Rules are available online at **www.gov.uk/check-an-employees-right-to-work-documents**. These rules are updated on a regular basis so it is worthwhile checking the site regularly for any changes to the rules relating to employing foreign workers.

If you employ, or plan to employ, people from outside the UK, you need to make sure that they have permission to work here before they start working for you.

Proof of entitlement to work in the UK

There are different types of documents that employers should check to ensure that their foreign employees are entitled to work in the UK. Employers who do not undertake these checks are liable to prosecution if they are found to be employing foreign nationals who are not entitled to work in the UK.

To be entitled to work in the UK, a foreign national must provide you with one of the following:

- a passport showing that the holder, or a person named in the passport as the child of the holder, is a British citizen or a citizen of the United Kingdom and Colonies having the right of abode in the United Kingdom
- a passport or national identity card showing that the holder, or a person named in the passport as the child of the holder, is a national of the European Economic Area or Switzerland
- a residence permit, registration certificate or document certifying or indicating permanent residence issued by the Home Office or the Border and Immigration Agency to a national of a European Economic Area country or Switzerland
- a permanent residence card issued by the Home Office or the Border and Immigration Agency to the family member of a national of a European Economic Area country or Switzerland
- a Biometric Immigration Document issued by the Border and Immigration Agency to the holder which indicates that the person named in it is allowed to stay indefinitely in the United Kingdom, or has no time limit on their stay in the United Kingdom
- a passport or other travel document endorsed to show that the holder is exempt from immigration control, is allowed to stay indefinitely in the United Kingdom, has the right of abode in the United Kingdom, or has no time limit on their stay in the United Kingdom
- an Immigration Status Document issued by the Home Office or the Border and Immigration Agency to the holder with an endorsement indicating that the person named in it is allowed to stay indefinitely in the United Kingdom or has no time limit on their stay in the United Kingdom, when produced in combination with an official document giving the person's permanent National Insurance Number and their name issued by a Government agency or a previous employer
- a full birth certificate issued in the United Kingdom which includes the name(s) of at least one of the holder's parents,

when produced in combination with an official document giving the person's permanent National Insurance Number and their name issued by a Government agency or a previous employer

- a full adoption certificate issued in the United Kingdom which includes the name(s) of at least one of the holder's adoptive parents, when produced in combination with an official document giving the person's permanent National Insurance Number and their name issued by a Government agency or a previous employer
- a birth certificate issued in the Channel Islands, the Isle of Man or Ireland, when produced in combination with an official document giving the person's permanent National Insurance Number and their name issued by a Government agency or a previous employer
- an adoption certificate issued in the Channel Islands, the Isle of Man or Ireland, when produced in combination with an official document giving the person's permanent National Insurance Number and their name issued by a Government agency or a previous employer
- a certificate of registration or naturalisation as a British citizen, when produced in combination with an official document giving the person's permanent National Insurance Number and their name issued by a Government agency or a previous employer
- a letter issued by the Home Office or the Border and Immigration Agency to the holder which indicates that the person named in it is allowed to stay indefinitely in the United Kingdom, when produced in combination with an official document giving the person's permanent National Insurance Number and their name issued by a Government agency or a previous employer.

All the documents that potential employees provide must be originals – photocopies, printouts or other copies are not acceptable. The process of checking that a worker is entitled to work in the UK is outlined in more detail in the Home Office publication *Prevention of Illegal Working: Comprehensive guidance for employers on illegal working* which can be downloaded from the Gov.uk website **www.gov.uk/government/publications/prevent-illegal-working-in-the-uk**.

Checking employees' documentation
It is your responsibility to look carefully at the documents that applicants provide and to ensure that, to the best of your ability, these documents are genuine and that the potential employee is entitled to work in the UK.

LICENCES & CONSENTS

MARKETING

GUESTS

FOOD & DRINK

HEALTH & SAFETY

STAFF

BUSINESS MANAGEMENT & TAX

FURTHER INFORMATION

Care should be taken over the following aspects of the documentation provided.

- **photographs** – does the person look like the photographs on their documents?
- **date of birth** – is the date consistent with the appearance of the candidate?
- **expiry dates** – are the documents still valid?
- **stamps and endorsements** – do the passport stamps allow your job applicant to do the type of work you are offering?
- **name** – is the same name used on all the documents?

When you have checked the candidate's documents and you are satisfied that they are genuine, you will need to save copies of them for your records either by photocopying or scanning the documents onto your computer.

The Public Register of Authentic Identification and Travel Documents Online (PRADO) can help you ascertain the authenticity of a document. Visit **www.prado.consilium.europa.eu**.

Penalties for non-compliance
Penalties include:

- civil penalties for employers who employ illegal migrant workers
- a criminal offence for knowingly employing illegal migrant workers, which carries a maximum two year prison sentence and/or an unlimited fine
- employers' continuing responsibility for checking the ongoing entitlement to work in the UK of migrant workers with a time-limited immigration status.

To avoid a civil penalty, you should check prospective employees' documents and undertake repeat document checks at least once a year for those employees who have limited leave to enter or remain in the United Kingdom.

Points-based migration system

The Government has introduced a points-based migration system for people from outside the European Union wanting to live and work in the UK. Migrants need to pass a points-based assessment before they are given permission to enter or remain in the United Kingdom. The tiers are:

- **Tier 1:** highly skilled, e.g. scientists or entrepreneurs.
- **Tier 2:** skilled workers with a job offer, e.g. nurses,

teachers and some chefs.

- **Tier 3:** currently suspended (low skilled workers filling specific temporary labour shortages, e.g. low-skill hospitality workers).
- **Tier 4:** students.
- **Tier 5:** youth mobility and temporary workers, e.g. working holidaymakers.

With the exception of Tier 1 workers, all other non-EU workers and students need a UK sponsor to vouch for them.

This points-based system ended previous employment routes to the UK for low-skilled workers from outside the EU, except in cases of short-term shortages. Therefore, unless the newly-formed Migration Advisory Committee identifies specific temporary shortages in the hospitality sector, most employment in the sector will have to be sourced from within the European Union.

Fees for sponsoring overseas workers

Businesses have to pay a one-off licence fee, which lasts for four years, to allow them to sponsor workers to come to the UK. For example, the licence fee for Tier 2 is £536 for businesses with fewer than 50 employees, and £1,476 for businesses with over 50 employees. (The fee is per business rather than per employee.) See the *UK Visa Sponsorship for Employers* section of the **www.gov.uk** website for more information.

Further guidance

- Further information on employing foreign nationals can be from the Visa and Immigration Section of the **www.gov.uk** website
- Alternatively, you can phone the UK Visa and Immigration helpline: 0300 123 4699 Monday to Thursday 09:00 - 17:00 and Friday 09:00 - 16:30
- *Prevention of Illegal Working: Comprehensive guidance for employers on illegal working* is available on the **www.gov.uk** website.

UPDATED

Employing Children

KEY FACTS

- There are special requirements that you must comply with if you are employing children under the age of 18.

- It is illegal to employ anyone under the age of 13 and children can only undertake full-time employment once they reach school-leaving age.

- Unless the child is a family member, you must undertake a separate Health and Safety Assessment of their position that takes into consideration their age and lack of experience.

- Children aged 16 and 17 are able to serve alcohol in a dining room or restaurant without supervision or behind a bar if each individual sale is approved by a responsible person.

The **Children (Protection at Work) Regulations 2000** were introduced to help ensure that children are protected in the workplace and that employers pay special attention to their safety and well-being.

Does this apply to me?

Yes: although there are some exemptions if you are employing a family member on an occasional or short-term basis.

Employing Children

It is not uncommon for small accommodation businesses to provide part-time or occasional employment to the children of friends and family. However, you need to be aware that there are a number of legal requirements and restrictions that govern the employment of children under the age of 18.

Generally, outside the performing arts, the youngest age a child can legally work part-time is 14, regardless of whether the payment for the work is monetary or in kind. However, this rule is often relaxed by byelaws so it is important to check with your local authority in order to determine the rules in your area.

Moreover, children can only start full-time work once they've reached the minimum school leaving age. They can then work up to a maximum of 40 hours a week.

School-aged children are not entitled to the National Minimum Wage. Young workers aged 16 to 17 are entitled to at least £3.72 per hour.

Hours of Work
For children who are over school leaving age and under 18, there are specific requirements relating to their hours of work. These employees must not work more than eight hours a day (or more than 40 hours a week) and there must be at least twelve hours' rest between each working day and 48 hours' rest per working week. You must also provide a 30-minute rest break when they work longer than four and a half hours.

Health and Safety
A child under 18 cannot be employed for work that:
- is beyond the child's physical or psychological capacity
- involves harmful exposure to toxic or carcinogenic substances
- involves harmful exposure to radiation
- involves a risk which cannot be recognised or avoided by young persons because of their lack of attention to safety, or lack of experience or training (this is likely to mean that any employment in kitchens involving the use of sharp knives or slicers will be prohibited)
- involves a risk to health from extreme cold or heat, noise or vibration.

If you are employing someone under 18, you must undertake a separate Health and Safety assessment, paying particular attention to their age and lack of experience. This does not apply if the child is a family member undertaking short term or occasional work.

If the child is under school-leaving age, you must also tell one of their parents the results of the assessment. This must include any risks identified and any measures you are putting in place to protect their health and safety at work.

Serving Alcohol
Under 18s can work in restaurants, dining rooms and even pubs, where they can wait on tables, collect glasses, clear tables and take orders from customers.

Children aged 16 or 17 are allowed to sell or serve alcohol in a restaurant without supervision provided that:
- it is sold or supplied to be drunk with a table meal, and that

- it is served in a part of the premises used only for that purpose.

This means that a child aged under school leaving age can work as a waiter or waitress in a dining room and serve alcohol without supervision.

Children can also work in a bar serving alcohol, as long as each individual sale has been specifically approved by a responsible person. The responsible person is either the holder of the Premises Licence, the Designated Premises Supervisor (DPS) or anyone aged 18 or over who has been authorised by the Premises Licence Holder or the DPS to authorise sales made by under 18s.

Note: you need to check whether your local authority has any bye-laws that restrict people aged under 18 selling alcohol. It is known that some local authorities prevent children under 18 selling alcohol that is not in a sealed container (e.g. unopened bottles or cans).

Further guidance

- The Government publication *Guidance on the Employment of Children* can be downloaded from the **www.gov.uk** website **www.gov.uk/government/uploads/system/ uploads/attachment_data/file/193326/Child_employme nt09.pdf**.

LICENCES & CONSENTS

MARKETING

GUESTS

FOOD & DRINK

HEALTH & SAFETY

STAFF

BUSINESS MANAGEMENT & TAX

FURTHER INFORMATION

Income Tax, VAT and Legal Form of Business

KEY FACTS

- You must establish your income tax position, and whether you are claiming all the expenses and capital allowances you are entitled to.

- There are different tax and legal implications depending on whether you operate your business as a sole trader, a limited company or a partnership.

- Tax and VAT are very large and complex areas of legislation that are constantly being revised and amended. For this reason we suggest that you contact your accountant or financial advisor to discuss all related issues.

Income tax

It is important that you establish your income tax position and whether you are claiming all the expenses and capital allowances you are entitled to claim.

Note: the Government has introduced a 'cash basis' tax scheme for self-employed individuals or partnerships carrying on the smallest trading businesses. Under this scheme, you can choose to be taxed on the basis of the receipts you gain minus the payments you make. You can join the scheme provided that your receipts for the year do not exceed the amount of the VAT registration threshold (currently £81,000) or twice that (currently £162,000) for recipients of Universal Credit. However, you must leave the scheme if your receipts exceed twice VAT registration threshold (currently £162,000). Further information is available at **www.gov.uk/simpler-income-tax-cash-basis/overview**.

You can speak to an accountant or a financial advisor, or visit HM Revenue and Customs website **www.hmrc.gov.uk**, which has a range of helpful information and contact numbers.

UPDATED

VAT

VAT Threshold

You do not have to register for VAT if your turnover for the previous 12 months is less than £81,000 (2014/15). This figure is known as the VAT registration threshold. The Government adjusts this figure each year so it is important to check on the HMRC website to find the current level.

You must also register for VAT if:
- you think your VAT taxable turnover may go over the threshold in the next 30 days alone
- you take over a VAT-registered business as a going concern.

VAT Deregistration Threshold

The deregistration threshold is £79,000 (2014/15). If your VAT taxable turnover for the year falls below £79,000, or you expect it to fall below £79,000 in the next 12 months, you can ask be deregistered for VAT.

Flat Rate VAT Scheme

If your VAT taxable turnover is less than £150,000, you can simplify your VAT accounting by calculating your VAT payments as a percentage of your total VAT-inclusive turnover. The current flat-rate VAT percentage for accommodation businesses is 10.5% of your VAT-inclusive turnover. Once you join the scheme you can stay in it until your total business income is more than £230,000.

It is recommended that you talk to your accountant as to whether joining the Flat Rate Scheme would be beneficial for your business.

For information go to The VAT Guide at **www.hmrc.gov.uk** or contact the HMRC's National Advice Service on 0845 010 9000.

Tax and your staff

For information on PAYE, National Insurance, download the Employer Further Guide to PAYE and NICs at **www.gov.uk/government/ uploads/system/uploads/attachment_data/file/300136/CWG2_ 2014.pdf**.

There is a range of guidance available from the HM Revenue & Customs on **www.hmrc.gov.uk** and you can also contact the HMRC's helpline: 0300 200 3200.

UPDATED

UPDATED

Legal form of the business

There are different tax and legal implications depending on whether you operate your business as a sole trader, a limited company or a partnership. There are advantages and disadvantages for each category.

You need to seek professional advice from lawyers or independent financial advisors – see the *Further Information* section, page 186.

Further guidance

To ensure you are not paying more taxes than required and understand the options available to you, VisitEngland has worked with HMRC to make available a range of free online learning resources, including step-by-step tutorials and webinars. For more information visit **http://www.hmrc.gov.uk/startingup/help-support.htm.**

LICENCES & CONSENTS

MARKETING

GUESTS

FOOD & DRINK

HEALTH & SAFETY

STAFF

BUSINESS MANAGEMENT & TAX

FURTHER INFORMATION

Tax Status of Accommodation Businesses

KEY FACTS

- In terms of taxation, there is a fundamental difference between the way HM Revenue and Customs (HMRC) treats holiday accommodation and standard rental properties.
- Having your property treated as a trade business, rather than a rental property, carries a number of advantages.
- To comply with the Furnished Holiday Letting Rules a property must be available for at least 210 days a year, let for at least 105 days and operated in a commercial manner.

Rental and trade businesses

In terms of taxation, there is a fundamental difference between the way HM Revenue and Customs (HMRC) treats holiday accommodation and standard rental properties.

- Rental properties are deemed to be *rental businesses*.
- Hotels, guest houses and B&Bs are treated as *trade businesses*.
- Self-catering accommodation can be treated as a trade business provided that the conditions of the 'Furnished Holiday Letting Rules' are met.

Having your property treated as a trade business carries the following advantages:

- it ensures that income, net of allowable expenses, is treated as earned income. This means that losses can be offset against other income (Note: this does not apply to self-catering properties) and capital allowances can be claimed in respect of all furniture and equipment used in the business. This compares favourably with the treatment of rental properties, where losses can only be offset against future income and you cannot claim capital allowances in respect to any new furniture and equipment.

LICENCES & CONSENTS

MARKETING

GUESTS

FOOD & DRINK

HEALTH & SAFETY

STAFF

BUSINESS MANAGEMENT & TAX

FURTHER INFORMATION

- trade businesses are treated as a business asset for the purposes of determining Capital Gains Tax, which gives you far greater allowances than you get for rental properties. Therefore, you pay less tax when you come to sell either the property or the business.
- for Inheritance Tax purposes, the property is deemed to be a business asset and can be passed on tax free.

Note: HMRC was recently successful in challenging the inheritance tax exemption of a self-catering property by arguing the level of service provided to guests was not sufficient for it to be deemed a trading business for the purposes of Inheritance Tax. You should therefore seek professional advice as to whether your property is exempt from inheritance tax.

Furnished Holiday Letting Rules

In order for your self-catering property to qualify as a trade business the following conditions need to be met:

1 **Commercial operation:** the business must be carried on commercially, and with a view to a profit.
2 **Pattern of occupation:** total periods of longer term occupation must not exceed 155 days (approx. 5 months) during the relevant period. A period of longer term occupation is a letting to the same person for longer than 31 continuous days.
3 **Availability:** the property must be available for commercial letting as holiday accommodation to the public for at least 210 days (approx. 7 months) during the relevant period.
4 **Letting:** the property must be commercially let as holiday accommodation to members of the public for at least 105 days during the relevant period. A letting for a period of longer term occupation is not a letting as holiday accommodation for the purposes of this condition.

The reason for these conditions is to prevent people from trying to gain trade business status, and the associated benefits, for either their home or their holiday home when they have no intention of operating them as a commercially viable bed and breakfast (B&B) or self-catering operation.

Note: It is important to note that if you operate a self-catering property, you are unable to claim sideways loss relief against other income. Also, regardless of complying with the FHL Rules, HMRC may deem your self-catering property to be subject to capital gains tax and inheritance tax if it is determined that you do not provide a sufficient level of services to demonstrate that it is a trading business. It is therefore important to gain advice from an accountant who understands the taxation rules for self-catering businesses.

Further guidance

The tax rules relating to holiday accommodation are complex, so it is best to seek advice from a professional tax consultant on the most efficient way to set up and operate your business.

LICENCES & CONSENTS

MARKETING

GUESTS

FOOD & DRINK

HEALTH & SAFETY

STAFF

BUSINESS MANAGEMENT & TAX

FURTHER INFORMATION

Business Rates

KEY FACTS

- Business rates generally apply to bed and breakfast establishments **unless** the business does not intend to offer short-stay accommodation to more than six people simultaneously **and** you occupy part of the property as your only or main home **and** letting out the rooms is subsidiary to the use of the rest of the house as your home.

- Business rates apply to a self-catering establishment **unless** you offer short-term lets for fewer than 140 days a year.

- Only the part of the property used for business purposes is subject to business rates.

- Your local authority will calculate the business rates for your property based on its 'rateable value'.

Do I need to pay business rates?

- **Yes:** if you are providing serviced or self-catering accommodation, unless:
- You qualify for Small Business Rate Relief, or

- **For bed and breakfast:**
  - you do not intend to offer short stay accommodation to more than six people simultaneously, and;
  - you (the owner) occupy part of the property as your only or main home, and;
  - letting out the rooms is subsidiary to the use of the rest of the house as your home ('subsidiary' is based on factors such as the length of your season, the scale of modifications undertaken for guests and the proportion of the house you occupy). For example, if you only let only two of six bedrooms in your property as a B&B, business rates are unlikely to apply. However, if you let four of your six bedrooms, you will probably have to pay business rates. Your local authority will be able to advise you.

UPDATED

- **For self-catering:**
  - you offer short period lets for fewer than 140 days a year. It is important to note that this is the period of the year when the property is available to be let, NOT the period over the year that it is let.

Note: if you have to pay business rates, but use your property for business and domestic purposes (a composite hereditament), it is only the part you use for business purposes that is subject to business rates. The domestic accommodation is liable to council tax. Where parts of a house have a shared use, such as a kitchen or dining room, the Valuation Officer will visit the property and assess the amount to be paid (see below).

Small Business Rate Relief
You can get small business rate relief if you only use one property and its rateable value is less than £12,000.

Until 31 March 2015, you'll get 100% relief (doubled from the usual rate of 50%) for properties with a rateable value of £6,000 or less. This means you won't pay business rates on properties with a rateable value of £6,000 or less. The rate of relief will gradually decrease from 100% to 0% for properties with a rateable value between £6,001 and £12,000.

If you have more than one property, you can get small business rate relief if the rateable value of each of your properties is less than £2,600. The rateable values of the properties are added together and the relief applied to the main property.

How are business rates calculated?

If you need to pay business rates, your property will have a 'rateable value' based on the rental value of your property. These values are set by an independent Government Agency, the Valuation Office Agency (VOA).

The Rateable Values of non-domestic properties are usually revised every five years. The last revaluation came into force on 1 April 2010 and is based on 1 April 2008 rental values. The next revision, which was due in 2015 and based upon 2013 rental values, has now been delayed until 2017 in both England and Wales. It is uncertain whether this review will result in an increase or a decrease in rates for accommodation businesses.

Your local authority will calculate your business rates by multiplying the rateable value of your property by a multiplier, or 'poundage', set

LICENCES & CONSENTS

MARKETING

GUESTS

FOOD & DRINK

HEALTH & SAFETY

STAFF

BUSINESS MANAGEMENT & TAX

FURTHER INFORMATION

each year by the Government.

You can obtain details of the rateable value of your property from your local Valuation Office or the business rates department of your local authority. The VOA website allows you to access entries in local rating lists: **www.voa.gov.uk/corporate/index.html**.

Transitional arrangements
There are transitional arrangements in operation which phase in the increase in business rates associated with the 1 April 2010 revaluation. This relief sets a limit to the percentage by which your business rate bill can increase each year until 2015.

The transitional relief is automatically included in the bill you receive from your local authority.

Lodging an appeal
You can make an appeal against the 2008 valuation of your property at any time during the life of the valuation (i.e. until 1 April, 2017). You are advised to appeal as soon as possible as you will have to pay your rates in full until a decision has been reached and, for most appeals, there are limits on how far any resulting change in value will be backdated.

Appeals are made in the form of a 'proposal' to the local Valuation Officer or online through the VOA website. If an agreement is not reached within three months of receipt of your proposal, it will be automatically referred to the local Valuation Tribunal, which will hear the case and give a decision.

Seeking the advice of commercial valuers
If you feel that the valuation of your business is too high, and you are not satisfied with the advice you have received from the local Valuation Officer, you may wish to consult a private firm of valuers or rating consultants before deciding to lodge an appeal.

Before agreeing to employ any rating consultants, always confirm:
- the terms
- their expertise
- their professional indemnity insurance cover.

Fees for commercial valuers
The fees paid should depend on the amount of work needed and on whether the appeal can be resolved by agreement. If a firm is handling a number of appeals from a specific area, it may negotiate a settlement that includes all of them, which will reduce the cost of each individual case.

Unfortunately there have been a number of reports of 'unqualified' firms seeking to obtain rating instructions by offering to represent ratepayers on payment of a fixed fee (payable before any work is done) and 'guaranteeing' a successful outcome to the appeal. Often cold calls are made by telephone or in person to the property and you are best advised not to employ such organisations. No one, no matter how eminent, skilled or experienced, can guarantee that an appeal will be successful.

It is also important to note that, although rare, it is possible for appeals to lead to an increase in the rateable value of your property (e.g. when the records of the Valuation Officer are not up-to-date on the physical extent of the property or the fact that it is being used for short-stay accommodation). Only reputable firms should be used to help you appeal against your rating assessment. Members of the Royal Institution of Chartered Surveyors (RICS) and the Institute of Revenues Rating and Valuation (IRRV) are regulated to protect the public from misconduct, and are required to hold adequate indemnity insurance.

Further guidance

- For information on the valuation of your property or appeals, contact your local Valuation Office (listed in the telephone directory), or visit their website: **www.voa.gov.uk/ corporate/index.html**.
- For any enquiries about your business rates bill, contact the business rates department of your local authority.
- Factsheets on the rules associated with the application of business rates to B&Bs and guesthouses, and self-catering properties are available on the 'publications' section of the VOA website.

LICENCES & CONSENTS

MARKETING

GUESTS

FOOD & DRINK

HEALTH & SAFETY

STAFF

BUSINESS MANAGEMENT & TAX

FURTHER INFORMATION

Self-Catering Letting Options

KEY FACTS

- You need to consider self-catering letting options if you let a property for holiday purposes.
- Occupiers do not gain any rights to stay on in your property as long as it is actually let for a holiday.
- For out-of-season lettings, you may wish to consider an assured tenancy or an assured shorthold tenancy.

Holiday letting

If you let a property for holiday purposes, the law allows you to do this without the occupiers gaining any rights to remain in the property. There is no limit to the length of the holiday let, but it must actually be for a holiday. 'Holiday letting' is defined in the **Housing Act 1988** as 'a tenancy the purpose of which is to confer on the tenant the right to occupy the dwelling house for a holiday'.

You are recommended to have a basic agreement with the occupiers (this can be by letter), which includes a statement that you are letting the premises as a holiday let, with the start and end days of the let clearly stated.

Note: while there is no limit to the length of a holiday let, to comply with the Furnished Holiday Letting Rules ((see *Tax Status of Accommodation Businesses*) the letting must not be for longer than 31 continuous days. Also, the Immigration Bill is currently being introduced which could require you to check the immigration status of guests staying for longer than three months to ensure that they are legally entitled to be in the country.

If the occupier doesn't leave at the end of the let, legally you don't have to go to court to recover possession of the property. However, you would still be strongly advised to apply to the Courts for eviction.

UPDATED

Out-of-season letting

If you are thinking of supplementing your income by letting your property for a number of months out-of-season, you can opt for:

- an assured tenancy
- an assured shorthold tenancy.

Assured tenancy

Assured tenancies are designed to give tenants the right to remain in your property until you have reason, or grounds, to seek possession. The relevant grounds in this case would be that the property has been let temporarily 'out of season' (such lets are often called 'winter lets', although they occur during any time of the year).

Setting up an assured tenancy

The let must be for a fixed period not exceeding eight months.

At some time in the 12 months leading up to the let, the property must have been occupied as a holiday letting, to indicate that this is the usual use of the property.

You must give the tenant written notice before the start of the tenancy (or include a simple declaration in the tenancy agreement) that says that the tenancy is not an assured shorthold tenancy and that possession might be recovered on the basis of Ground 3 of the Grounds for Possession in the **Housing Act 1988**.

Ending an assured tenancy

You have the right to seek possession of the property at the end of the fixed period of the tenancy.

To bring the letting to an end, you give the tenant two weeks' notice, using a special form, to coincide with the end of the fixed term. If the tenant does not leave at the end of the notice, you would have to start court proceedings to recover possession of the property.

Assured shorthold tenancy

A simpler form of assured tenancy that many landlords prefer to use is an assured shorthold tenancy. This allows you to seek possession even when there is no specific grounds for you to do so. However, this would mean that the tenant has the right to stay in the property on this basis for a minimum of six months (even if you have agreed a fixed term for less) or the length of the fixed term, whichever is the longer.

There are no special procedures for setting up a shorthold tenancy, but you must give two months' written notice to seek repossession.

If the notice period expires and the tenant doesn't leave, you must still recover possession through the Courts. However, for recovering possession on a 'no-ground' assured shorthold basis, you can use the Accelerated Possession Procedure, which can be quicker and cheaper than a full court hearing.

Alternatively, you can set up a fixed-term out-of-season assured shorthold tenancy, by prior notice to the tenant, as for a full assured tenancy.

Note: remember that planning restrictions may have been imposed on you as a condition of permission being granted for the property's use as a holiday property.

Further guidance

- You should always take legal advice before you enter into any tenancy agreement
- The publication *Assured and Assured Shorthold Tenancies – A Guide for Landlords* can be downloaded from **www.gov.uk**.

Houses in Multiple Occupation

KEY FACTS

- In some cases, your local authority may class your accommodation as a House in Multiple Occupation (HMO).
- If you feel that your property is being classed wrongly as an HMO by the local authority, you may appeal to a residential property tribunal.
- HMOs usually need to be licensed by the council.
- Environmental Health Officers are responsible for enforcing HMO legislation locally.

In a few local authority areas, guest houses, bed and breakfasts and holiday flats have been classed as HMOs. When this happens, the implications for a proprietor can be far reaching.

The **Housing Act 2004** introduced mandatory licensing and a new definition of HMOs.

What is an HMO?

A house in multiple occupation is defined in the Housing Act 2004 as:

- an entire house or flat that is let to three or more tenants who form two or more households and who share a kitchen, bathroom, or toilet facilities
- a house that has been converted entirely into bedsits or other non-self-contained accommodation and which is let to three or more tenants who form two or more households and who share kitchen, bathroom, or toilet facilities
- a converted house that contains one or more flats that are not wholly self-contained (i.e. the flat does not contain a kitchen, bathroom and toilet) and that is occupied by three or more tenants who form two or more households
- a building that is converted entirely into self-contained flats if the conversion did not meet the standards of the **Building Regulations 1991**, and more than one third of the flats are let on short-term tenancies.

Tenants

In order to be an HMO, the property must be used as the tenants' only or main residence and it should be used solely or mainly to house tenants. Properties let to students and migrant workers will be treated as their only or main residence and the same will apply to properties which are used as domestic refuges.

Therefore, holiday cottages let to families or other groups of people living together as one household for a holiday, who have a main home elsewhere, are not HMOs.

Where winter letting to groups of people who are not related is taking place, the premises may well be considered to be an HMO and you should seek advice.

What being an HMO means

Owners who intend anything other than holiday letting should seek advice and talk to their local authority. If the premises are deemed to be an HMO, they will have to meet some strict standards concerning amenities and fire precautions in the building. Usually they will need to be licensed.

The great majority of holiday homes are not HMOs. Bed and breakfast accommodation may be if it is let to people who don't have another residence.

Licensing

Under the national mandatory licensing scheme, an HMO needs to be licensed if it is a building consisting of three or more storeys and is occupied by five or more tenants in two or more households.

The council will grant a licence to an HMO if it is satisfied that:
- the HMO is reasonably suitable for occupation by the number of people allowed under the licence
- the proposed licence holder is a 'fit and proper person'
- the proposed licence holder is the most appropriate person to hold the licence
- the proposed manager, if there is one, is a 'fit and proper person'
- the proposed management arrangements are satisfactory
- the person involved in the management of the HMO is competent
- the financial structures for the management are suitable.

Enforcement

Environmental health officers, who are responsible for enforcing

HMO legislation locally, have the right to enter a property at any reasonable time after giving 24 hours notice in writing. Also, they may serve legal notices requiring the provision or improvement of amenities.

Standards

Properties of the relevant type must be licensed throughout the UK, while local authorities have discretion to adopt additional licensing schemes in regard to lower-risk properties. Before granting a licence, they will need to be satisfied that a set of standards are met. If they are not met, they will judge the property not to be reasonably suitable and refuse to grant the licence.

The standards come from a Government circular. Most local authorities adopt similar sets of standards, but there are variations. The standards include requirements for fire precautions. See the *Fire Safety (General)* section.

Appeals

If you feel that your property is being classed wrongly as an HMO by the local authority, you may appeal to a residential property tribunal.

Further guidance

- Detailed advice on all of the above is available from local environmental health officers for the area in which the property is situated. They are contactable through the local authority.
- Further information on HMOs is available at **www.gov.uk/private-renting/houses-in-multiple-occupation**.

LICENCES & CONSENTS

MARKETING

GUESTS

FOOD & DRINK

HEALTH & SAFETY

STAFF

BUSINESS MANAGEMENT & TAX

FURTHER INFORMATION

UPDATED

Utilities and Waste Collection

KEY FACTS

- If the water supplies for your accommodation come from a private supply, the **Private Water Supplies Regulations 2009** apply to you.

- Local authorities must take and analyse samples of private water supplies from groundwater sources.

- If you make a specific charge to your customers for gas or electricity, the most you can charge is limited by the 'maximum resale price' rule.

- The maximum resale price is the same price that you have paid to your own supplier.

- If you pay business rates, you need to pay for a commercial waste collection service unless you are exempt under the Controlled Waste Regulations 2012.

Private water supplies

Private water supplies include water:
- from groundwater sources
- drawn from privately owned boreholes or wells
- taken from surface water, such as springs and streams.

The **Private Water Supplies Regulations (England) 2009,** together with the **Water Industry Act 1991**, apply to all private water supplies intended for human consumption, whether this is for drinking, washing or food production. The aim of the regulations is to ensure that all private water sources are safe and free from contaminants.

Do these Regulations affect me?
Yes: if any part of the water supply for your accommodation business comes from a private supply.

Private water supply tests
The 2009 Regulations require that each local authority must record the number of private supplies in its area, and for each supply

must record:

- the name of the supply, together with a unique identifier
- the type of source
- the geographical location, using a grid reference
- an estimate of the number of people supplied
- an estimate of the average daily volume of water supplied in cubic metres
- the type of premises supplied
- detail of any treatment process, together with its location
- the name of the Health Protection Agency in whose area the supply is located.

After the initial assessment, the Regulations require local authorities to monitor the supply on an ongoing basis. The regularity of the sampling will vary depending upon the volume of water used, from once a year for supplies of less than 10 cubic metres per day to 34 times a year for supplies of up to 10,000 cubic metres per day.

In addition, the local authority must also undertake a thorough risk assessment of each supply at least once every five years.

Cost of samples

The local authority will contact the person responsible for the supply (this may be the landowner, a person using the water, or a person representing a group of water users) about sampling. The Regulations set out the maximum amounts that a local authority can charge for undertaking risk assessments, taking and analysing samples and providing authorisations to use a private water supply.

The bill will be sent to the person responsible. If an authority decides to carry out tests over and above those required by the regulations, it has to bear the costs of these tests itself.

If test results show that the water is unwholesome, because it fails to meet the standards or other requirements, the local authority can insist the water supply is improved. If any private supply of water intended for human consumption constitutes a potential danger to human health, a local authority acting under these Regulations will serve a notice to the responsible person. It is an offence to breach this notice. However, the Regulations establish an appeal process if you wish to challenge a notice.

The resale of gas and electricity

Maximum resale prices

If you are reselling gas and/or electricity that has already been bought from an authorised supplier, the amount you can charge your customers is limited by the 'maximum resale price rule'. This means that the most you can charge a customer for the supply of gas or electricity is the amount that you yourself have been charged by your gas or electricity supply company. Put another way, you can only sell gas or electricity to your guests on a non-profit basis.

As the provisions relating to the maximum resale prices for electricity and gas are reviewed from time to time, you should also occasionally check the Ofgem website (see Further guidance below) to see whether there have been any changes.

Do maximum resale prices apply to me?

- **Yes:** if you make a specific charge to your customers for gas or electricity, whether or not you use individual meters to record their consumption. The rule typically applies to self-catering accommodation and caravan sites, although it affects all forms of accommodation where separate charging occurs. If you overcharge for electricity or gas, your customer can ask for a refund of the excess and can pursue the matter in the small claims courts if necessary.

- **No:** if you do not make a specific charge for electricity and/or gas (e.g. if customers are charged a single rental figure for fully inclusive accommodation). The rule also does not apply to any gas or electricity that is used in communal facilities, e.g. for the use of a dryer in a laundry room or a shower in a washroom block at a caravan park. In other words, there is no maximum limit on what you can charge a guest for using a communal washing machine, provided that this use is billed separately to the charge for general gas and electricity use.

Price of energy units

If you are charged a **single unit rate** for gas or electricity by your own supplier, you must charge your customers the same rate. If the unit rate varies, e.g. if you pay on an economy 7 type tariff, or prices vary on a seasonal basis, you will need to calculate an average price for each unit used.

A copy of the explanatory publication, *The Resale of Gas and Electricity – Guidance for Resellers* is available to download from the Ofgem website **www.ofgem.gov.uk**. This gives further information and includes example resale price calculations.

Standing charges

In addition to the charge for units used, many authorised suppliers levy a standing charge to cover the cost of maintaining your connection and billing you for the fuel. You can recover this from your customers – the individual sums need to be calculated according to the number of units of electricity used by each consumer. Once again, the Ofgem publication gives further guidance.

Waste Collection

If you pay business rates then, unless you qualify for an exemption under the Controlled Waste Regulations 2012, you will need to pay for a commercial waste collection service either through your council or with a private contractor. The Controlled Waste Regulations provide an exemption from waste disposal charges for small businesses that:

- were operating prior to 6 April 2012 and were eligible for free waste disposal at this date; and
- are eligible for Small Business Rate Relief (i.e. the property has a rateable value of less than £12,000).

Note: waste collection charges comprise of two components – a charge to collect the waste and a separate charge to dispose of the waste. Therefore, even if you qualify for the exemption from waste disposal charges, you will still need to pay for your waste to be collected.

Further guidance

- Advice on private water supplies is available through the environmental health department of your local authority.
- The Drinking Water Inspectorate (DWI) publication *Keeping your private water supply safe* can be downloaded from their website **www.dwi.defra.gov.uk**.
- More detailed technical advice for professionals who are involved in treatment and assessment of private supplies is set out in the DWI technical manual available on their website.
- Information on waste collection, including eligibility for an exemption under the Controlled Waste Regulations is available from your local authority.
- *The Resale of Gas and Electricity – Guidance for Resellers* gives further information and includes example resale price calculations. It is free to download from Ofgem **www.ofgem.gov.uk**.
- Ofgem will also answer any specific queries which cannot be resolved via their website.

Government and Public Bodies

National government level

There is a variety of sources of information and advice available from Government. Some general sources are given below.

Open government

All government departments are migrating their websites to a single entry point to all UK public sector information **www.gov.uk**. This website replaces Government Direct and Business Link.

VisitEngland

VisitEngland, the national tourist board for England, also provides market intelligence and business support tools online free of charge: **www.visitengland.com/businessadvice**.

Destination Organisations (DOs)

The structure and function of local tourist organisations vary from region to region, but supporting local tourism businesses is a common priority. They may offer a number of services that can help you, including:

- information and guidance about starting up a tourism business (several offer more extensive business support services)
- training courses
- appropriate marketing opportunities
- general information on tourism within their area, development plans, local tourism trends and statistics.

They can also act as a signpost, directing you to other regional and local bodies that you need to contact or that can offer you further assistance.

Note: Some of these services may be restricted to members.

Other National Tourist Boards

- VisitScotland
  www.visitscotland.org
- Visit Wales
  www.visitwales.com
- Discover Northern Ireland
  www.discovernorthernireland.com

- VisitGuernsey
  www.visitguernsey.com
- Isle of Man Tourism
  www.visitisleofman.com
- Jersey Tourism
  www.jersey.com

Note: VisitBritain **www.visitbritain.org** is the national tourism agency, responsible for promoting Britain worldwide and developing its visitor economy.

Local sources of help and advice
Contacting your local authority
Throughout this publication, we suggest that you contact your local authority for additional help and advice. If you live within the administrative area of a metropolitan borough council, unitary council or London borough council, then you have a single point of contact for your enquiry.

Alternatively, if you live in an area which has both a borough/district council and county council, then it is advisable to first call your local borough/district council with your enquiry.

Other sources of local help
These include the following:

Tourism officer
Most local authorities have a dedicated officer responsible for tourism promotion, who is able to offer a wide range of information on issues affecting the local industry. These areas of expertise include environmental health, licensing requirements, local sustainable tourism, marketing initiatives, quality assurance, and tourism trends and statistics.

Tourist Information Centre (TIC)
Your local TIC is another source of valuable information as the staff have a detailed local knowledge of the locality. For instance, they are uniquely aware about the types of visitors who visit the area and their requirements of small tourism business.

Business Support Helpline
The helpline provides a quick response service if you have simple questions about starting or running a business. It also provides a more in-depth service if you have more complex enquiries.
- Telephone: 0300 456 3565. Monday to Friday, 9am - 6pm.

Local libraries

Your local library (or the nearest town/city library) is also a good source of advice and information on local matters and government initiatives. They may also have copies of some of the publications mentioned in this booklet.

Local tourism partnerships/initiatives

In certain parts of the country local authorities have come together, often in partnership with local tourism businesses, to form a local tourism marketing group or initiative. Your local DMO will be able to tell you about groups and initiatives in your area and how to contact them for more information.

Other sources of help

Legal advisors

The Law Society is able to provide you with a list of solicitors within your area. Your local DMO may also be able to give you names of suitable local firms **www.lawsociety.org.uk**.

Independent financial advisors

The IFA consumer website is able to forward you a list of independent financial advisors, accountants or solicitor in your area **www.unbiased.co.uk**.

Utilities/facilities

These include the following:

Gas Safe Register

- Telephone: 0800 408 5500
- **www.gassaferegister.co.uk**

OFGEM (The Office of Gas and Electricity Markets)

- **www.ofgem.gov.uk**

OFCOM (Office of Communications)

- Telephone: 0300 123 3333
- **www.ofcom.org.uk**

OFWAT (Office of Water Services)

- Telephone: 0121 644 7500
- **www.ofwat.gov.uk**

Trade associations

These include the following:

Bed and Breakfast Association

- Telephone: 01935 815252
- **www.bandbassociation.org**

British Activity Providers Association

The BAPA monitors safety standards and quality within the activity sector throughout the British Isles. BAPA also provides a detailed consumer guide which is available on request.

- Telephone: 01746 769982
- **www.thebapa.org.uk**

British Holiday and Home Parks Association

BHHPA is the representative body of the parks industry including caravans, chalets and tents and all types of self-catering park accommodation.

- Telephone: 01452 526911
- **www.bhhpa.org.uk**

British Hospitality Association

The BHA represents hotels (mostly 10+ rooms), restaurants and catering establishments, and distributes guidance notes to members.

- Telephone: 020 7404 7744
- **www.bha.org.uk**

British Destinations

British Destinations represents the interests of resorts and destinations throughout the UK.

- Telephone: 0151 934 2285 / 2286
- **www.britishdestinations.co.uk**

English Association of Self-Catering Operators

The EASCO is a trade association for self-catering operators from individual owners through to the agencies and associations.

- Telephone: 020 7078 7329
- **www.englishselfcatering.co.uk**

Farm Stay UK Ltd

Farm Stay UK Ltd is a co-operative of 1,200 farmers throughout the UK who provide serviced and self-catering accommodation on working farms.

- Telephone: 024 7669 6909
- **www.farmstayuk.co.uk**

Tourism for All

Tourism for All, a national charity, is the UK's central source of travel and holiday information for disabled people, older people and carers.

- 0845 124 9971
- **www.tourismforall.org.uk**

People 1st

People 1st is the Sector Skills Council for the hospitality and tourism sector. It is the lead agency on all issues relating to education, training and qualification within the sector.

- Telephone: 0870 060 2550
- **www.people1st.co.uk**

National Caravan Council

NCC is the representative trade body for the UK caravan industry involved in setting standards and promoting quality. NCC operates the Product Approval Scheme for new caravans to ensure compliance with minimum health and safety standards.

- Telephone: 01252 318251
- **www.thencc.org.uk**.

Business advice

VisitEngland's industry website features a business advice hub with a wide range of tailored guidance, tools and resources, including The Pink Book Online, best practice editorial features and an Online Marketing Toolkit **www.visitengland.com/businessadvice**.

Business skills

Business advice, including training, funding finance and IT is available from a wide range of government-related organisations and websites including:

- **www.learndirect.com** on 0800 101 901
- Business Helpline on 0300 456 3565
- **www.gov.uk/business**
- your local council
- your local Destination Management Organisation

Environment and energy helpline

Contact **www.wrap.org.uk** or phone 0808 100 2040.

Tourism trends in your area

Contact your local DMO, your local tourist information centre, or your local authority tourism officer.

VisitEngland also provides market intelligence online free of charge on their industry website.

Marketing opportunities

Contact your local DMO, any local tourism marketing initiative, or your local authority tourism officer.

Publications Contact List

The publications mentioned within individual legislation sections are available from the following organisations:

Advisory, Conciliation and Arbitration Services (ACAS)

- National helpline: 08457 474 747
- Orderline: 0870 242 9090
- **www.acas.org.uk**

Advertising Standards Authority (ASA)

- Orderline: 020 7492 2222
- Online order: **www.asa.org.uk**

Department for Business, Innovation and Skills

- 1 Victoria Street, London SW1H 0ET
- Telephone: 020 7215 5000
- **www.gov.uk/government/organisations/department-for-business-innovation-skills**

Department for Communities and Local Government

- Eland House, Bressenden Place, London SWLE 5DU
- Telephone: 0303 444 0000
- **www.gov.uk/government/organisations/department-for-communities-and-local-government**

Department for Culture, Media and Sport

- 100 Parliament Street, London SW1A 2BQ
- Telephone: 020 7211 6000
- **www.gov.uk/government/organisations/department-for-culture-media-sport**

Department for Environment, Food and Rural Affairs

- Nobel House. 17 Smith Square, London SW1P 3JR
- Telephone: 08459 33 55 77
- **www.gov.uk/government/organisations/department-for-environment-food-rural-affairs**

Department for Transport

- Great Minster House, 33 Horseferry Road, London SW1P 4DR
- Telephone: 0300 330 3000
- **www.dft.gov.uk**

Department of Health

- Richmond House, 79 Whitehall, London SW1A 2NS
- Telephone: 020 7210 4850
- **www.gov.uk/government/organisations/department-of-health**

Equality and Human Rights Commission

- Telephone: 0808 800 0082
- **www.equalityhumanrights.com**

Food Standards Agency

- Aviation House, 125 Kingsway, London WC2B 6NH
- Telephone: 020 7276 8829
- **www.food.gov.uk**

Health and Safety Executive

- Redgrave Court, Merton Road, Bootle, Merseyside L20 7HS
- **www.hse.gov.uk**

Incident Contact Centre on 0845 300 9923 *Note: this can only be used to report serious or fatal accidents.*

HM Revenue and Customs
- VAT Helpline: 0845 010 9000
- Employer Helpline: 08457 143 143
- **www.hmrc.gov.uk**

Home Office
- 2 Marsham Street, London SW1P 4DF
- Telephone: 020 7035 4848
- **www.gov.uk/government/organisations/home-office**

Information Commissioner's Office
- Wycliffe House, Water Lane, Wilmslow, Cheshire SK9 5AF
- Helpline: 0303 123 1113
- **www.ico.gov.uk**

Pay and Work Rights Helpline
- Telephone: 0800 917 2368
- **www.gov.uk/pay-and-work-rights-helpline**

Office of Fair Trading
- Fleetbank House, 2-6 Salisbury Square, London EC4Y 8JX
- Telephone: 08454 040506
- **www.oft.gov.uk**

TSO (formerly The Stationery Office)
- TSO Customer Services, PO Box 29, Norwich NR3 1GN
- Orderline: 0870 600 5522
- **www.tsoshop.co.uk**

Trading Standards Institute
- Consumer Direct helpline: 08454 04 05 06
- **www.tradingstandards.gov.uk**

Valuation Office Agency
The VOA is now an agency of HMRC.
- England - 03000 501 501
- Wales - 03000 505 505
- **www.voa.gov.uk**

Definitions and Explanations

The following definitions aim to clarify terms used throughout the text.

Employer
Anyone who has employees, whether through a written contract or a simple verbal agreement.

Employee
Anyone who works for you under a contract of employment. This may be a formal written contract, or it may be an oral agreement, or even just implied.

Note: in some instances deciding whether someone is an employee can be a complex area of law (e.g. if you hire someone who is self-employed and they have little or no other employment, they may be deemed to be your employee). Professional legal help is recommended if you are uncertain.

Hotel and private hotel

The term 'hotel' can be used in its everyday, general sense. However, it is also a term defined under the Hotel Proprietors Act 1956 to clarify certain rights and responsibilities that are attached to being a Hotel (as defined), rather than any other type of accommodation premises. These rights and responsibilities include (a) a responsibility for guest's luggage and belongings, (b) the right to keep guests luggage, and (c) the right to turn guests away.

For these purposes:
A hotel is an establishment that offers (i) food, (ii) drink, (iii) sleeping accommodation, to anybody who appears able and willing to pay and who is in a fit state to be received.

Note: 'drink' does not have to be alcoholic.

A private hotel is any serviced accommodation establishment that is not a hotel. For example, you will be a private hotel if:
- you do not provide food and/or drink
- you can pick and choose your guests, even if you have a free room
- you have an advertised policy of 'no children' or 'no coaches', etc
- you can only book in advance.

Serviced accommodation

Includes hotels, hostels, guest houses, bed and breakfasts, farmhouses and inns.

'So far as is reasonably practicable'

This phrase occurs frequently in health and safety legislation. It means that you have to do what is reasonable taking account of the level of the risk and the time, trouble and expense involved in removing or minimising it. If the risk is low, it is not reasonable to commit significant resources. If the risk is higher, it is reasonable to have to commit significant resources. For example, if your property is old with low door frames and beams, there is a high risk of someone banging their head but a low risk of someone being seriously injured, it is therefore reasonably practicable for you to put up warnings, but not to structurally alter the premises.

It is important to note that this phrase does not pertain to your financial circumstances (i.e. it is not a defence to say that you did not undertake reasonable measures to ensure the safety of guests or staff because you couldn't afford them).

Star ratings

Since 2006 the assessing bodies (mentioned below) have reached agreement on what is known as 'Common Standards'. Not only will they assess serviced and self-catering accommodation to the same criteria, but this also ends the confusion previously caused by crowns, diamonds, stars, keys, ticks, to name a few of the previous symbols.

Stars ratings denote the quality rating achieved and designators (e.g. town house hotel, metro hotel, restaurant with rooms, guest house) will give customers additional information to help them find the style of accommodation they want. The aim is to reduce confusion and avoid misleading the customer.

Choice of assessing body

Four agencies currently offer this service:

- VisitEngland
- the AA
- VisitScotland
- Visit Wales.

Quality assessment means that an independent assessor has visited every year, supplied a written report and, in the case of hotels and B&Bs, has stayed overnight as a 'mystery' guest at least one year in three.

To find out more, contact the relevant organisation below.

VisitEngland quality contact

Quality in Tourism (for assessments in England only)
1320 Montpellier Court
Pioneer Way
Gloucester Business Park
Gloucester GL3 4AH
- Telephone: 0845 300 6996
- **www.qualityintourism.com**
- Email: qualityintourism@uk.g4s.com

VisitScotland quality contact

Quality and Standards
Thistle House
Beechwood Park
North Inverness IV2 3ED
- Telephone: 01463 723040
- **www.visitscotland.com/quality-assurance**

- Email: qainfo@visitscotland.com

Visit Wales quality contact

Ty Glyndwr
Forge Road
Machynlleth
Powys SY20 8WW
- Telephone: 0845 0108020
- **www.wales.gov.uk/tourism**
- Email: tourism.industryadvice@wales.gsi.gov.uk

The AA

14th Floor
Fanum House
Basing View
Basingstoke RG21 4EA
- Telephone: 01256 493835
- **www.theaa.com/hotel/hotel_services_index.html**

VisitEngland's Quality Assessment Schemes

VisitEngland has invested heavily in its own Quality Assessment Schemes, which are available to all accommodation and attraction operators in England. For the accommodation sector, the administration and assessing has been contracted to Quality in Tourism, who operate the different schemes on VisitEngland's behalf.

A range of accommodation schemes are available covering:
- hotels
- guest accommodation
- budget hotel brands
- holiday villages
- holiday, touring and camping parks
- self-catering accommodation serviced apartments
- boats
- hostels.

Around 17,000 businesses currently participate in the accommodation scheme.

VisitEngland quality ratings

Each scheme awards stars (1-5) to give a clear indication of the accommodation standard, taking into account the cleanliness, facilities, hospitality, service and food. The ratings provide visitors with the reassurance they need to help them choose their accommodation. Generally, the more stars, the higher the quality of accommodation.

Designators such as 'town house hotel', 'country house hotel' and 'restaurant with rooms' give visitors even clearer information when making their choice.

Visitor attractions

A visitor attraction quality assessment scheme is also in operation, delivered in England by a professional team of VisitEngland assessors.

This consumer-focused quality assessment of visitor attractions helps to identify the strengths of an attraction and highlights development areas, based on industry examples. A wide range of attractions throughout England of all sizes, both large and small, have benefited from participation in the service.

For further information please go to **www.visitengland.com/businessadvice** or email attractions@visitengland.org. For attractions in Scotland and Wales, please contact the relevant national tourist board – see VisitScotland quality contact and Visit Wales quality contact above.

Index

Legislation in *italics*
Major page references in **bold**

A

The AA 192, 193
ACAS (Advisory, Conciliation and Arbitration Service) 141, 155, 188
access statement 65–6
accidents
    duty of care 91, 108
    reporting 96, **100**, 101
    slips and trips 108, **110–11**, 113, 120
accommodation
    accepting guests **57–9**
    accommodation offset 144
    bookings contract 40–1, 51–2, 53
    cancelled bookings 40–1, 53–6
    deposits 54, 55
    disabled guests 58–9, 60
    food and drink 74, 76
    houses in multiple occupation 126, **177–9**
    letting options 174–6
    out-of-season letting 176, 178
    package holiday regulations **37–9**
    pricing and charging 50–2
    tax status **167–9**
    unfair comparisons 28
    unfair trading practices 27
    utility supplies **180–3**
adoption leave 153, **153**
Adventure Activities Licensing Regulations 2004 121, **122–3**
Adventure Activities Licensing Service 123, 124
advertisements
    Data Protection Act 44
    signage 22
    unfair trading practices 27–8, 29–30, 50
    see also marketing
Advertising Standards Authority (ASA) 189
age discrimination 150
agency workers 99–100
alcohol **1–8**, 162
allergies **81**, 83, 85–6
alterations to buildings 18, 19, 127–8
animals 57, 63

B

babies
    baby-listening services 72
    baby-sitting 72
    breastfeeding 149
    maternity/paternity leave **151–5**
bed and breakfast
    accommodation
    business rates 170, 173
    houses in multiple occupation 177, 178
    tax status 167
bedsits 177
belongings
    retaining 57, **69–70**
    rights and responsibilities 67–70
bills, non-payment 69–70
bonds 51–2
bookings contract **40–1**, 51–2, 53, 57
    see also lettings agencies
British Sign Language 64
Building Regulations 1991 177
Building Regulations 2000 18
building regulations **16**, 18, **19**, 109
Business Link 184
business management
    business rates **170–3**
    help and advice 184–5, 188–90
    houses in multiple occupation **177–9**
    income tax 164, 165–6
    legal form of business **166**
    self-catering letting options **174–6**
    starting up 83, 184–5, 188–90
    tax status of accommodation 167–9
    utility suppliers **180–3**
    VAT **165**
Business Protection from Misleading Marketing Regulations 2008 26, 28
business rates **170–3**, 183
Business Support Helpline 185, 188

C

cancelled bookings 40–1, **53–6**
capital gains tax 168–9
caravans 9, 188
carers, discrimination 62
catering industry
    food hygiene **74–83**
    health and safety 89, 101, 106
    starting a business 83
caving 122
CCTV 4
change of use 16–18, 19
charging **50–2**, 53, 69–70
children
    childcare **71–3**
    employment 161–3
    health and safety 91, 98, 101, 122–3
    hotel bookings 58, 59, 67
    maternity/paternity leave **151–5**
    premises licence 5, 7
Children Act 1989 71–2
Children (Protection at Work) Regulations 2000 161
cleaning materials 78, 105–7, 127
climbing 122
coaches, private hotels 58, 67
cold callers 112
Community and Ancillary Sales Notices (CANs) 1
computers
    Data Protection Act 44
    data security 47–8
    health and safety 102, **103**, 106, 127
Conservation Areas, signage 24
The Consumer Contracts (Information, Cancellation and Additional Charges) Regulations 2013 31, 35
The Consumer Protection Regulations 2008 (CPRs) 22
The Consumer Protection (Distance Selling) Regulations 2000 31, 35
The Consumer Protection (Distance Selling) (Amendment) Regulations 2005 35
The Consumer Protection from Unfair Trading Regulations 2008 (CPRs) 26, 30, 50, 51
Control of Asbestos Regulations 2006 20
Control of Substances Hazardous to Health Regulations 2002 (COSHH) **105–6**, 107